MANAGING PEOPLE IN THE NEW NORMAL

Principles Based on Mental Health and Wellbeing

R I C H I E   P E R E R A

BALBOA.PRESS
A DIVISION OF HAY HOUSE

Balboa Press books may be ordered through booksellers or by contacting:

Balboa Press
A Division of Hay House
1663 Liberty Drive
Bloomington, IN 47403
www.balboapress.co.uk
UK TFN: 0800 0148647 (Toll Free inside the UK)
UK Local: (02) 0369 56325 (+44 20 3695 6325 from outside the UK)

Print information available on the last page.

ISBN: 978-1-9822-8654-5 (sc)
ISBN: 978-1-9822-8656-9 (hc)
ISBN: 978-1-9822-8655-2 (e)

Balboa Press rev. date: 12/02/2022

DEDICATION

I dedicate this book to my parents, Piyal Perera and Lilani Perera.

To my father, for his intelligence, passion for reading, diligent attention to detail, and meticulous organisation. His belief in accepting things as they are and enjoying a peaceful life in the hope of all things to fall into place for the better. If I had one wish, it would be for you to be alive to read your son's book.

To my mother, whose drive, determination, ambition, and work ethic is a phenomenon I am yet to witness in another human, along with her inability to take "no" for an answer. Thank you for all the doors you've opened for your family and many others.

A collective of characteristics and traits my parents blessed me with in good balance, allowing me to succeed at anything I put my mind to.

Thank you for everything.

SPECIAL THANKS

To my good friend and mentor, Graham Shapiro, a person who never misses the opportunity to tell me that I'm one of the most inspirational people he knows. A person who listened intently to my story and the challenges I've faced, then looked me straight in the eyes and responded, "I just can't wait to see what you do next." Thank you for being an amazing friend and mentor.

To my brother from another mother, Jerome Thomas. A person who showed me when life has dealt you the worst hand possible, a person can carry on fighting every day to maintain a good heart and be true and loyal to the people you love. You're truly one of a kind. I know it can never be, but I wish I could see your face when you first read this!

And, last but not least, to my long-time female best friend and now fiancé, Dijana Zimonja. I recognise how much it takes to put up with someone like me, well at least I try to. Being friends was much easier than being in a relationship. Little did we know.

Thank you for being the extreme opposite of me and finding joy and beauty in the smallest of things, helping to keep me grounded. Thank you for all the meals, teas, coffees, and prompts to drink water throughout the months of writing this book and in everyday life. Thank you for your gentle frequent reminders that I work in mental health, and I need to practice what I preach. Therefore, perhaps, that's enough working, screen time, and writing for today!

EPIGRAPH

"Because after all, every management that we do
is only for human wellbeing." – *Sadhguru*

ABOUT THE AUTHOR

Richie was formerly the founder and CEO of the London Makeup School and the London Hair Academy; his professional career is connected to BBC 1's Apprentice and highlighted by the Eden Project in Cornwall. The Business Matters Magazine has spotlighted his leadership as a CEO. Richie has sat as Chair of the Judging Panel at the IBX Awards in Dubai and worked as an expert industry consultant for Guidepoint Global. Richie won the highly acclaimed Investors in People Manager of the Year Award in 2018, recognising Richie as a global leader in HR and people management practices. After being diagnosed with and recovering from mixed depression and anxiety disorder, Richie founded

Mental Health and Life, an organisation that delivers mental health first aid courses alongside HR consultancy, race equity, and suicide intervention courses to individuals, organisations, and businesses UK-wide. Richie regularly writes articles on mental health and people management; his articles have been published by The Industry Leaders and the Employee Experience Magazine. Richie is an executive contributor at Brainz magazine and sits as deputy chair on the Board of Trustees at Unity Theatre in Liverpool.

1

There Are No Experts in the New Normal!

As a reader of this book, the first thing you must come to terms with is that in the working world, there are no experts for this new normal of ours. Well, at least not in 2022, when this book is due to be published. There won't be any experts for at least the next three to five years. This is because all major developments and challenges taking place in the working world are brand new. There's no businessperson or consultant alive who has experience with what's currently happening within the working world. This is great news for us all!

The changes happening in the working world are so new they're happening even as I write this book. When we use the term "new normal," none of us knows what that is or what it will look like. It's a term we've coined to describe the state we find ourselves post-pandemic, a description or prediction of how things may unfold. We know there's a new normal, but the conditions are still under construction. Hence, there are no experts, just a bunch of people trying to figure out what the best way forward could be or should be.

If you're in the UK, consider the implications of Brexit on the working world, especially if you're an employer. Brexit and the pandemic almost happened back-to-back. For organisations, it changed the way they operate, recruit, and manage people, permanently changing workplace culture. Some organisations are trying to return to how everything worked pre-pandemic. This, however, is only because they lack critical thinkers and opportunity spotters in their leadership. They are the dinosaurs of the new normal. Other organisations with forward-thinking leaders see the opportunities the new normal renders. They plan to change with the times and leverage the opportunity the new normal presents for sustainability, as they foresee, they have no actual choice.

Worldwide, the new normal presents organisations with a unique, once-in-a-lifetime opportunity and platform. One we'll probably never see again in our lifetimes. There's an opportunity for us to become experts and consultants in our management, both on a personal and professional level. The two are linked inextricably, a fact traditionally missed by employers while managing people. The new normal provides every person of working age the opportunity to affect workplace culture and influence workplace change for the better.

We must grab this opportunity by the horns, take control, and run with it. If we do, we'll have the power to bring about a revolutionary change in the working world for the better. The power to create a major positive impact on organisational behaviour and employee satisfaction worldwide that will benefit generations to come. An opportunity to change the status quo of the workplace, an opportunity so powerful it can rapidly pick up people and economies worldwide post-pandemic.

Change is a good thing; organisations need to embrace it, and the new normal is all about change management. The new normal has provided an opportunity to re-evaluate the role of HR, people management, organisational wellbeing, and behaviour. An opportunity to implement a new chain of thought that is a two-way street, mutually beneficial to both the employer and employee. Some employers and managers may think, people management and organisational wellbeing aren't a priority on this side of the pandemic. It's more about finances, survival, and getting the organisation back on its feet. I have a question for those who see things this way.

How can you have a healthy, sustainable organisation, without a healthy workforce?

If you have the answer to that question, you can stop reading this book.

Perhaps the time has even come to rename Human Resources (HR). Should humans be labelled a resource, like they're something to be mined? How about Human Relations or the Human Wellbeing Department? Just some food for thought. A triviality, it could be perceived, however, the incoming workforce of Gen Zs may have a different take on that. They are the future of all organisations. Organisations must be cognizant of the fact that stability is inextricably linked to employee wellbeing. It always has been, even more so now in the new normal.

Employers must shroud new people management practices and frameworks developed for the new normal in a cloak of wellbeing. Employers will need to acknowledge that true guidance and consultancy for success and sustainability sit right under their noses. It's called the workforce. Since cost saving in the new normal is so crucial for organisations, why spend money on external consultants when they can do the initial work for organisational stability internally and for free?

In the new normal, organisations won't find better consultancy than through the people already incumbent in an organisation. All they require is a safe space to be consultants. Employees within organisations should represent the primary form of guidance for their management and development. That's the future. When I started to write this book in 2021, there were developments unfolding that were both good and bad for the new working world. It was in the media constantly. As we exited the pandemic, I came across business decisions made by out-of-touch decision-makers that were obviously and painfully knee-jerk and short-sighted. I also found impressive, progressive, and inclusive decisions made by in-touch CEOs and senior managers. Decisions that were in line with the direction the new normal is heading. The decisions and the pathways organisations take with people management will ultimately make, or break, organisations in the new normal.

The decisions made now, good or bad, will become a part of the new working world currently under construction. Some organisations are already making huge errors which will haunt them, eventually. Particularly those with a top-down, "we here at the top know best," approach to how things operate in the new normal. The lockdown made some organisations conclude they no longer need their premises, working from home was all that was required. It's understandable why an organisation would make such a decision. Commercial space is one of the biggest overheads and headaches for any organisation. The option to operate without such a large overhead makes perfect financial sense. The problem is that decisions are only being made with financial sense, not with common sense, and there will be trouble ahead.

Since the pandemic and the transition to hybrid working, I've spoken with and trained many organisations, speaking with employees ranging from CEOs to office juniors, before, during and post-lockdown. I would estimate around half of the employees enjoy working from home, while the other half scream to get back to the office. There are so many variables as to why a person prefers home to the office and vice versa. A lot of these variables involve personal preferences and individual life factors. Some people want to get out as they need the physical movement, routine, and social interactions that come with going in to work. Others love working in their dressing gowns and having all the creature comforts of their home to hand. The future is a mix of both. Hybrid working is the "happy place" where all needs can be met. Organisations in the new normal must seek opportunities in hybrid working and leverage them.

There are many positives to hybrid working, along with some pitfalls employers need to keep in mind with health and safety.

- How are organisations monitoring wellbeing and supporting employees while working from home?
- What management practices have employers established to keep tabs on burnout, overworking, mental health, and work-life balance with remote working?
- How much people management is happening face to face, rather than over Zoom and Teams?

These are important talking points for organisations and challenges that need to be met head-on. If an employee burns out due to not receiving training on how to have a good work-life balance, how to shut down after work, how to stay active, and what to do to maintain their physical and mental wellbeing while working from home by their employer, the employer will be liable. With remote working, employers need to consider all health and safety aspects as they'd be considered within the office environment. This goes as far as having correct lighting, correct seating, and desks. Sit-Stand desks are an absolute must for hybrid working as pointed out by a colleague Steve Carr of Mindcanyon, who informed me of Dr Marie Pasinski's work. According to Dr Marie Pasinski, M.D. Professor of Neurology at Harvard Medical School, neurologist, and brain health expert, "prolonged sitting takes a profound toll on your brain – simply getting up every half hour for 2 minutes improves brain blood flow and metabolism, promoting new connections and new neurons. Set a timer or a fitness band 'idle alert' to keep you on your toes!" Are organisations passing on such crucial snippets of information regarding health and safety in the new normal? Organisations unconcerned with staff working at their dining tables and on their sofas may be liable for any health issues that come with it.

The best practice in the new normal would be to install, or offer to install, all the correct equipment for an employee's remote working environment. Training on how staff can serve themselves physically and mentally should be standard. Employers should purchase desks that offer both sitting and standing working options or standing desk converters. British Telecom (BT) raised prices because of a 90% increase in broadband services. With the current cost-of-living crisis, should organisations contribute to Wi-Fi and electric bills in the new normal? How about putting tracking systems into place, not to ensure contracted hours are being met, which would be an invasion of a person's home and privacy, but to prevent unsafe working practices such as working over contracted hours and late into the evenings? Both of which can lead to legal issues for the employer.

Aviva, a British multinational insurance company, found that around two in five people said they couldn't switch off from work. "One result of this always-on, ever-present culture is that 40% of employees are concerned about work-related burnout," the insurer said. Fifty per cent of people complained that the boundary between work and home had become "increasingly blurred," disproportionately affecting women, with 46%

concerned about burnout – compared to 35% of men. If employers don't put processes into place urgently, to mitigate the risks of remote working, it will eventually lead to legal claims and issues for employers. Employers need to remember their responsibilities for health and safety in the remote/hybrid working environment are the same as their responsibilities in the office environment.

Decisions by employers to go fully remote are usually based on an over-focus on financials. The belief that cost-cutting is the key factor to getting an organisation back on its feet can be regressive, rather than progressive. These decision-makers overlook the fact that to get an organisation back on its feet, employees need to be back on their feet first. These decisions are replicated at a political level, too. The focus is on getting the economy back on track, and getting things up and running, with no real regard for the health of the workers who are the beating heart of any economy. Politics or businesses, it's all leadership or the lack of it. These leaders haven't stopped to consider how people are feeling after the pandemic and lockdown. They have no real plan of action for it, just keen to crack the whip and get on with it.

There's also remote working loneliness to consider, especially for those living alone. The Mental Health Foundation reported that levels of loneliness tripled during the pandemic and that one-third of adults in the UK would never admit to feeling lonely. In the UK, 25% of people feel ashamed about being lonely. The UK government estimates that loneliness is connected to staff turnover, lower well-being, and productivity, currently costing £2.5 billion a year for employers.

There's a lack of consideration regarding all the trauma we experienced through the lockdown and pandemic. A lack of consideration for what many people are still experiencing. For the government and many organisations, "mental health" has become a buzzword, a good soundbite and a superlative to repeat when the opportunity arises. A perfect example of that in the UK was when teachers were told to get back to school and get on with the curriculum post-lockdown. There was no consideration of what happened to the children or the teachers during the lockdown. Decisions that were made by a political leadership overrun with dinosaurs, and completely out of touch with the wellbeing and social issues of the electorate.

There was no process or conversation around the most basic, yet most fundamental, of human needs, post-lockdown. No process to discover if both teachers and pupils were in a good mental state, coming out of the biggest disruption to everyday life since World War II. Teachers were just told to get on with it. Many organisations proceeded to follow the government's lack of critical thinking when they asked employees to return to work post-lockdown. Mental Health First Aid England (MHFAE) reported in March 2022, that almost half (48%) of employees had no wellbeing check from their employer in the past year. The report also found that, alarmingly, it was a backwards trend as only 25% went without a wellbeing check, in 2021.

When you consider that 50% of all mental health issues develop by the age of fourteen and two-thirds by the age of twenty-three in the UK, these statistics highlight that the family home and establishments that cater for these age groups have an extra and crucial obligation of addressing mental health and wellbeing. This has always been the case, long before the pandemic. This data and information should be common knowledge for decision-makers in government, especially since the 5–23-year-old age group is the main end user of the teaching and education sector. It's highly unlikely these statistics miraculously improved over the lockdown and pandemic, for children and young people.

In fact, they didn't, according to the National Health Service (NHS) as reported in September 2021.

- 1 in 6 children in England has a probable mental health disorder
- 39% of 6–16-year-olds experienced a deterioration in mental health from 2017–2021
- 53% of 17–23-year-olds experienced deterioration in mental health from 2017–2021

We know that during the pandemic, many people lost loved ones. I lost my father. Many people lost their jobs, many people faced financial issues leading to family and social problems. Mental health issues in children and adults skyrocketed, and anti-depressant use in both adults and children rose to record levels, as did alcohol and substance misuse, along with domestic abuse cases. In fact, 1 in 8 people in the UK are on anti-depressants, with 83.4 million anti-depressant items subscribed to the British public between 2021–2022. This isn't an exhaustive list of the consequences associated with the pandemic, which affected the mental health and well-being of both the children and teachers.

Instead of the government and leadership in the educational sector foreseeing that well-being will undoubtedly worsen over the lockdown and establishing a process to address it. Teachers were told to get back to work and get on with the curriculum. Some organisations have made the same mistake. This lack of critical thinking in a country as bright and productive as the UK, brings into question, how we managed to get so far economically with such a lack of critical thinking in our leadership, both in government and business. It also brings to question how much better we could be economically, with the right leaders in place, alongside healthy employees in the right state of mind.

In an alternative reality, with all the dinosaurs in leadership being extinct. The first month of teachers returning to school could've been spent on coping and resilience skills training, alongside mental health first aid and wellbeing training. This training would've provided information to establish a support framework for both children and teachers as they got back into the business of schooling. That support system would've been specific to each school, or even to each classroom, addressing its own unique challenges, making it an invaluable tool. This process, or something similar, should've been funded by the government regardless of the cost, as the proactive approach will always be more cost-efficient long term, than a reactive one.

Regardless of the money the government would've spent on funding this process, not spending will cost a lot more in the future. That isn't rocket science, it's simple risk management and common sense. Employees who are literate and possess skills in risk management, wellbeing and common sense, are key qualities that organisations need to be on the lookout for in the new normal. Deloitte reported in January 2020 pre-pandemic, that for every £1 an organisation spends on mental health interventions in the workplace; the ROI is £5. As a successful and award-winning CEO, I can safely say that any CEO/manager/decision maker worth their weight in salt, will know that this isn't a cost, but a solid investment. Anything that gives you a five-fold return is money well invested. In fact, it's a revenue stream.

Organisations that are not proactive with mental health post-pandemic, may be due to a generational issue. Managers that fall into Gen X and Boomer cohorts have their generational preconceptions regarding mental health, these preconceptions can be outdated and toxic in today's world. Now, this isn't necessarily the fault of Gen X and Boomers. They are, however, the two generations currently at the top of the food chain with organisational hierarchy. These two generations are the main decision-makers in the working world.

As a Gen Xer myself, I grew up when mental health wasn't a big topic, or maybe it was, but it wasn't mainstream like it is now. I grew up in a generation where I don't remember coming across the term mental health at school, college, or even in my early working years in my twenties. Not that mental health didn't exist. I remember there were many "nutters," "psychos," and people that had gone "bonkers" around. I used to hear about them all the time. It was only when one of my best friends and the father of my godson took his life by throwing himself under a train, that I paid more attention.

In those days, no one knew how to deal with a friend that was "normal" one minute and "mad" the next. School or college didn't teach us how to help someone mentally unwell, it just wasn't a topic we discussed in the 90s. I'm sure this terminology of "nutters," "psychos," and people that had gone "bonkers" has made a few readers in my generation giggle as they read it. Growing up, this terminology was based on ridicule. In those days, that's just how we dealt with it, by laughing it off, pretending it doesn't exist, and telling ourselves it's not our problem. Before my friend became mentally ill, my perception of "those people" was that they were beyond help, were dangerous, and had to be dealt with in a safe environment by professionals. As a generation, we weren't mentally literate enough to understand there's a huge space for education, understanding, help, and support between "normal" and "mad." Those days, it was more, you are "normal," or you are "mad," and no in-between.

What I do recall in hindsight, whenever I felt down at certain stages of my life, I was told to "man up," "stop being a girl," "sort yourself out," and "pull yourself together." Personally, for me and many from my generation and cultural background, this terminology created a stigma about showing emotion. It felt embarrassing, like it was a weakness. This narrative and approach to mental health is a common factor amongst the Gen X and Boomer generations. This ideology can be dangerously carried into the current working world, and we all need to be mindful of it.

In one of my mental health first aid courses, an older gentleman who was a senior HR business partner in a large multinational made a bold statement. He said "Why is mental health such a big thing now? Why didn't we have all the issues every young person seems to have now? Sometimes it feels like it's all just an excuse for lazy millennials looking to get a day off." As a mental health first aid instructor, I'm not someone to disregard a person's viewpoint. In today's world, a comment like this would get a person cancelled. This "cancel culture" has gone a little too far and has become damaging to society and in certain circumstances, it's become a tool for oppression. I prefer to provide information that may change a viewpoint or help a person re-evaluate their opinions, rather than cancel them. All the while understanding that even then, a person may not have the critical thinking skills to dissect an alternative viewpoint.

I explained to my learner it was simply because the generations that came after us grew up in an entirely different world. Older generations never faced the pressures the younger generation has. The fact is, Gen Xers and Boomers grew up in much simpler times and didn't have the digital stressors younger people grow up with, that impact mental health. The pressures of smartphones, social media, and the internet are aspects older generations didn't have to deal with as children and young adults. The world has also rapidly changed since the 1990s, with older generations telling the younger generations to go to school, work hard, and get a good job and everything will be fine. Those days are long over, the primary and secondary education system is archaic and has no relevance to the world young people enter after their schooling. Wages have hardly risen yet prices of everything have shot up. There's a good chance a lot of young working people won't get the opportunity to rent a decent home, let alone buy a house or even retire with any degree of comfort.

As a Gen Xer, if I was getting bullied at school, that stopped once I left school to go home. I would get an overnight break until school the next day, giving me some respite. In the world of millennials and Gen Zs, that bullying can carry on twenty-four hours a day with no relief via a mobile phone or social media. Can you acknowledge the difference in the impact? If you're Gen X and above, imagine your bully coming everywhere with you. They're at school, they're in your home, they're in your garden, they're in your bed. They also have a much larger audience liking and commenting on the skills of your bully. Can you imagine that and how that might affect you?

This pressure is just the tip of the iceberg younger generations face, and older generations struggle to comprehend. Older generations struggle to acknowledge why the younger generations are struggling with their mental health and asking for the support they deserve, both in life and within the workplace. I say to the older generation, don't try to understand, it's a waste of energy better spent elsewhere. It's the same as asking a Gen Z or a millennial to understand how it felt having no internet, no emails, using typewriters and faxes, landline phones, and having only four channels on TV. Could they understand those days or understand the mental health issues we faced in that era?

The older generation must realise that issues with young people's mental health are real, and it is happening. Then, make space for it within homes and places of work. Once we do, perhaps the older generations can learn something from it. The irony is, men aged 40–50 years old fall into the category with the highest rate of suicide in the UK. The highest rate of suicide in women happens to be those aged 45-49 years old. Therefore, maybe it's time for the older generation to park our preconceptions on mental health and pay more attention to what the young are saying!

This brings us to the important topic of actively listening, so we can learn how to understand and respond appropriately. These days we are all too easily offended, and we're all desperate to be right. Social media has played a major role where people take sides online and refuse to consider an alternative narrative or perspective. Everyone knows what they know, and they're right, the end!

This approach causes polarisation, keeping us angry and distrustful of one another. As long as we stay divided and unable to communicate, we'll never flourish. Let's keep in mind if someone is offended, that doesn't automatically make them right or a victim. The person who offended isn't automatically wrong and a perpetrator. This thinking and the cancel culture are cancerous in society and must be done away with. There must always be a space for dialogue and reasoning. We cannot get away from our different viewpoints due to our individual filters on reality. It's what makes us human. It's a cause for celebration, not division.

The way I planned my response to my learner shed light on the matter, leading him to apologise for his comment. I wasn't looking for an apology. My job as a trainer is to provide information, and I did just that. He was surprised he also fell into the category with the highest suicide rate. He was unaware it was such an issue in his age group, thus changing his position on how young people address mental health. Admitting when you're wrong is a brave thing to do. Being open to taking on and considering new information is a skill lacking in many.

We seem to live in a world where we don't want to be wrong or change our minds. Sometimes we prefer to go with what we feel, rather than the facts. Today, a lot of our information comes as memes, TikToks, and online opinions. They contain a combination of disinformation and misinformation, creating a breeding ground for ignorance and a safe space for everyone, no matter where you stand on an issue. This results in the inability to listen and learn from each other, which is fundamental to civilization. We then become so preoccupied with being right, or being on the right side, that we become unable to listen or accept anything new or entertain an opposing viewpoint. Some people don't want to stand corrected. It can be scary to reconsider what you think you already know or to stand corrected. It takes people out of their comfort zone. Ignorance is bliss, as the saying goes, but it's still ignorance.

We listen to, respond, like, or comment rather than to understand, then move on as quickly as we can. When we listen, we're already planning a response in our head, creating further disengagement from what a person is putting forward. Engaging with others in this way goes against our human nature. It's been created by a media overload, platforming short-sighted viewpoints by so-called experts with it all figured out. People naturally like to listen to narratives they want to hear, rather than what they need to hear. No one likes to be wrong, so it's important to be on the right side. How we conclude right and wrong leaves a lot to be desired on many topics we face in the world today. We must ask ourselves a fundamental question:

If we cancel correction and relearning, how will we ever learn anything new?

As humans, we need to be careful not to get stuck in a mindset that won't allow correction and reconsideration. A mindset where a person is incapable of learning something new because of flaws in their listening skills, leading to flaws in their critical thinking. In society, and within organisations, this leads to the blind leading the blind. The ability to take on new narratives and perspectives is essential in the new normal. Mindsets and cultures within organisations can be changed by providing new information that can change organisational behaviour for the better. This, however, can only happen if organisations will entertain new narratives and perspectives, instead of thinking what they're doing is still competent.

The aim of this book is to change organisational behaviour by changing the mindsets of working people. In the everyday world, we may have the luxury of choosing not to socialise with a person incapable of considering a new narrative or taking on an alternative perspective. If you're surrounded by such people on a social level, it will be hard to grow as a person. We like to describe such people as "stuck in a rut." On a social level, we can simply move on, being mindful that we're not the person who lacks perspective and critical thinking. Self-awareness is everything!

In business, however, we lose the luxury of being able to just move on. Managers unable to listen, think critically, and understand new information, negatively affect those they manage. Business leaders and managers who enjoy continuously learning and unlearning are essential in the new normal. Being wrong is a good thing if you can accept it. When you're wrong and are provided with new information and corrected, you've learned something new. That shouldn't be a source of shame. As Einstein said, "Once you stop learning, you start dying."

This image is a perfect example of how we, as humans, view the world based on our individual filters on reality and where we stand through lived experience. So much so, that if a group of people were locked in the same pitch-black room for 24 hours, their individual experiences will all be different, with some commonalities here and there. If you asked a group of people to walk to a window, stand for two seconds, and then write one thing they saw, they'd all write different things, even though they stood at the same window for the same time. I learned this fact when the instructor of my training as a mental health first aider asked my group to do the same. The view out the window was mostly the side of another building, nothing more than windows and drainpipes. I was in a group of eight, and it was eye-opening all the different things spotted by the group. Almost everyone saw something different, with some similarities. It made me wonder how reliable an eyewitness can be!

Organisations, managers, and leaders must understand this aspect of human nature to manage people better. Once we do that, we realise our differences are a part and parcel of being human, something to be celebrated and in a professional environment, managed, and leveraged. In the world, our differences are pitted against us. From the colour of our skin to our religions, genders, and political views. The list goes on.

So, instead of uniting, understanding, and celebrating our differences, we are divided, distrustful, and even hateful. I am a firm believer that being in any group other than humanity is a bad place to be. Once we accept our differences make us human, and that we all see, feel, and understand things differently. We can change the way we are with each other. It will help us be kinder to each other and that is essential for our wellbeing. As people, we must be aware we all carry a burden on our shoulders and that being kind costs nothing. We all have the superhuman ability to raise another person with something simple as a "hello," a compliment, or even just a smile!

In the new normal, we need to use that superhuman ability for its intended purpose, to raise each other up. On an organisational level, this can be as simple as sending an email with common courtesy. Start an email with, "I hope you had a good weekend," if it's a Monday, "Enjoy your weekend," if it is a Friday, and so on. Even if you must speak to a member of staff about a gripe you have with them, start with your emails in this manner. When you do, it will naturally tone down a harsh email you've written by bringing in a human element, essential in the new normal.

From speaking with my clients, emails between managers and staff are one of the main stressors for an employee's workday. In the new normal, we must remember not to forget our basic manners and etiquette. In the same way, you wouldn't walk up to a person or an employee, instruct them, and walk off without a hello or a goodbye. Your email etiquette needs to be mindful of those same basic manners and principles. In our new world of hybrid working, where more engagement is happening digitally, manners and etiquette do maketh the manager!

On the flip side of our superhuman ability to raise others, we also have a dark ability to ruin someone's day with a poorly thought-out remark or email. The person or situation that ticked you off at work. The email you then sent in a bad mood (I've made this mistake as a CEO when the pressure became too much). That person who cut you up on the road making you fly into a rage and swear at them. Your harsh comment or angry rant could lead to someone having a terrible week, or worse, attempting suicide. Be mindful that your poorly conceived, off-the-cuff comment or email could be the straw that breaks the camel's back for that person. As a society, we're doing this way too much, in the workplace, online, with our families, and in social circles. We don't know what a person could be going through. Your comment could easily tip a person over the edge, especially on this side of the pandemic.

The next time you get irate with another person in your personal or professional life, ask yourself, "is this the end of the world?" Can you let this go or rethink your response for your sake and theirs? Are you able to take a second and become more self-aware in your response? What you'll notice is that in nine out of ten situations that may arise, you can let go, walk away, or handle them in a better way. A lot of situations in daily life and at work are fleeting moments; if you don't react, they remain a fleeting moment. You'll also feel better for not reacting in a bad way. It will prevent you from upsetting yourself and another person. There's a certain peace in that. Try it, it feels great, and it's contagious!

When we accept each other's differences as a natural human element, we then realise we have more in common than not. It doesn't matter who you are and where you're from. We're all humans with fears, hopes, dreams, and aspirations. Our work as humans is to support each other with these basic needs and help each other overcome our fears. Nurture is a fundamental element of our human essence. It's vital in the new normal that organisations recognise this, as it's the same with the relationship between employer and employee. On the most basic level, an employee working for a company contributes to the growth and success of that business. The growth and success of the business is the dream and aspiration of the business owner or shareholders. The employee is helping to nurture and achieve that dream for them. So why are so many organisations not reciprocating?

Paying an employee, a wage they can live on with dignity, offering a good benefits package, a decent holiday allowance and one that increases annually. At least forty wellbeing hours a year, where an employee can take time out for themselves when they need to, during working hours that does not impact pay, and a decent paternity/maternity leave is the absolute minimum an employer must provide. Beyond this minimum to further support employees, internal training and continuous professional development (CPD) are a must, so employees can continue contributing to the organisation. Taking interest in an employee's personal goals and ambitions, and supporting employees to achieve them, is the new outlook for great people management. It's time for organisations to throw out the old HR and people management rule books, they are no longer fit for purpose and develop new ones.

If you are a shareholder, CEO, or business owner, ask yourself if this is the way your organisation is set up. Look at the lowest-paid people in your organisation and ask yourself if you could raise your family on the same wage and benefit package. If you can't, urgent changes need to take place within your organisation. In fact, this isn't your decision to make. That decision was made for you, as you'll discover further in this book. Whenever I consult organisations on this topic, I use my family car analogy. Please don't assume I'm comparing cars to humans here; however, it will make sense to you as a reader or a leader.

A CEO is buying a family car and requires the car to get from A to B. To do that safely, the car must have:

- A good foundation; its tyres and engine
- An MOT (British annual check of vehicle safety)
- Regular servicing
- Insurance
- Road Tax (dependent on its size and capacity)
- Fuel to run and function

All the above comes at a cost. Once covered, you have a sturdy, trusted, and reliable motor that can take you from A to B safely. Now, if you ignore any of these requirements, the car will give you problems. It may become unreliable and a source of shame. It could also get you into trouble with the authorities.

Now, let's consider employees, as they require the same level of care and service to function. You'll see below how the need for a reliable car relates to the needs of a reliable employee:

- A good foundation; its tyres and engine - Equivalent to a thoughtful and supportive employer
- The MOT - Equivalent to a good framework for mental health and wellbeing
- Regular servicing - Equivalent to a robust and supportive appraisal framework, EAP, and people management practices
- Insurance - Equivalent to CPD and robust health and safety procedures
- Road Tax - Equivalent to manageable workloads depending on the capacity of the individual
- Fuel to run and function - Equivalent to a decent living wage and benefit package

The difference between a car and an employee is that one is a machine, and the other is a living, breathing human. The next big difference is that no matter how well that car is cared for and looked after, it will depreciate year on year. Period, as the Americans say. The car will always be a depreciating asset, but an employee isn't. An employee is only ever a depreciating asset if the organisation allows them to be. If you work in an organisation where employees are underperforming, it may be time to look at the functions of the organisation, rather than the employee, to address it. Organisations need to realise that employees are an infinite source of appreciation if they are managed well.

An employee who is well serviced is an appreciating asset. With good leadership and management, an employee can be supported to increase their productivity and performance by at least 10% year on year. This will have a positive impact on the bottom line of the organisation. It will help the organisation grow in areas outside of its financials and, inadvertently, come back around to have a positive impact on its financials. Servicing aspects such as workplace wellbeing, happiness, and a healthy culture will attract and retain the best talent. It will help an organisation manifest a core set of vision and values needed for sustainability in the new normal. How can that not be a dream or aspiration for any organisation post-pandemic?

I ask CEOs, leaders, and decision-makers in business reading this book, why do you look after your family car so well even though it's a depreciating asset, yet you're not too keen to invest in servicing your employees, who are an appreciating asset and a solid investment in the future of your organisation? The same asset that helped you to afford your family car in the first place and live the life you do. Can you make it make sense?

Over the pandemic, we witnessed the richest, most powerful organisations in the world become even richer. In fact, the pandemic saw one of the greatest wealth transfers in history, from poor to rich. According to OXFAM International, the ten richest men saw their fortunes double from $700 billion to $1.5 trillion. To put this into perspective their wealth grew at a rate of $15,000 per second or $1.3 billion a day. This happened during the first two years of the pandemic which saw 99% of income fall globally and over 160 million more people forced into poverty.

Some of these organisations are notorious for paying low wages, using zero-hour contracts, treating their staff as expendable, and grinding them into the ground, thus contributing to poor health and social issues throughout the world. I don't have to name these organisations; we all know who they are. They're the organisations now richer than ever, with all that extra profit they made because of the pandemic. Ecstatic with their strategy of low wages, zero-hour contracts, and no benefits, during the most miserable time in living memory for most. As they pat themselves on their backs for a job well done, they've overlooked a critical flaw in their strategy. They didn't stop to consider the profitability that could've been leveraged by treating their employees with the dignity they deserved, making sure they were properly looked after before, during, and post-pandemic. This may have created some extra overheads, but at a negligible cost when compared to the potential billions to gain long term. I say to these organisations, it's still not too late!

One of the best changes an organisation can adopt is getting a new perspective on people management and ridding itself of its dinosaurs. Dinosaurs in organisations are people who don't possess the thinking skills required for sustainability in the new normal. These relics have played a major part in the "problem" of how organisations behaved in the past. They have no place in our future. This brings us back to the opportunity we have in the new normal. New perspectives will mean doing something that sends shock waves through some managers and organisations. They'll need to talk to their employees!

So, what is the "problem" that organisations need to be mindful of, you may ask?

The problem is as follows (UK Based):

- Deloitte in January 2020 (pre-pandemic) reported that employers were losing £45 billion every year because of mental health issues at work. Rising £6 billion every year since 2016. That cost stands at £56 billion in 2022.
- Poor mental health carries an economic and social cost of £105 billion a year in England, and £10.8 billion a year in Scotland. Around 595,000 workers experienced work-related stress, depression, or anxiety in the UK.
- 15.4 million working were days lost due to work-related stress, depression, or anxiety.
- Working days lost due to stress, depression, or anxiety accounted for 57% of all working days lost because of ill health. The primary cause of work-related stress, depression, or anxiety was due to people's "workload," accounting for 44% of all cases.

The problem is as follows (U.S. Based):

- 83% of U.S. workers experience work-related stress.
- U.S. businesses lose up to $300 billion yearly because of workplace stress.
- Stress causes around one million workers to miss work every day.
- Only 43% of U.S. employees think their employers care about their work-life balance.
- Depression leads to $51 billion in costs because of absenteeism and $26 billion in treatment costs.
- Work-related stress causes 120,000 deaths and results in $190 billion in healthcare costs yearly.

Looking at such statistics, it's hard to believe this was happening pre-pandemic, yet many organisations are reverting to this defunct, pre-pandemic style of people management and operations, with the same leaders and thinking that manufactured these statistics. It's nothing but organisational self-harm. The statistics show we were functioning with a broken and sick workforce. It's surprising the economy somehow grew pre-pandemic when you consider the mental state and health of the UK and U.S. workforces. The statistics emphasise how tough humans are and highlight how much more we'd be capable of, if we got health and wellbeing right in the workplace.

Organisations reverting to their old ways have made a huge mistake. These organisations will eventually hit an iceberg and go the same way the Titanic did. They are doomed and led with the same arrogance that gave rise to the claim that the Titanic was unsinkable. We all know how that turned out. These are the same employers and managers who think, people management, and organisational wellbeing aren't a priority in the new normal, they see training in these areas as a tick-box exercise. Does that remind you of yourself or the management and leadership team within your organisation? If so, you now know your dinosaurs.

Getting to know your employees, both on a personal and professional level, is the future of people management. This is essential for employers to understand, as truly flourishing profits and productivity can only be achieved with a truly healthy and flourishing workforce. The challenges and opportunities we face in people management are brand new; we're all learning on the job. It's a great time for great change and the ability to influence it. In this new normal, every organisation must work out what is best for them. There's no generic solution, only a unique one.

What must not happen is reverting to broken people management practices, which never truly leveraged the workforce. It would be insanity to conclude what didn't work pre-pandemic, will somehow and miraculously, work post-pandemic. Further considerations for organisations to contemplate are the experiences of employees during the lockdown.

Alliance Care, a global healthcare solutions provider, reported:

- January 2021 was the saddest on record for the UK, beating a previous low in 2012, when the country faced the first double-dip recession since the 1970s.

Workplace wellness statistics from Champion Health, a digital employee wellbeing platform, showed:

- 90% of UK employees thought the pandemic affected their mental health
- 40% said it had a moderate or significant impact on their wellbeing
- 60% experienced symptoms of depression
- 26% experienced moderate-to-severe levels of anxiety in 2020

The Office for National Statistics (ONS) in the UK suggests these figures are likely to increase in 2021, revealing that 42% of adults had reported high levels of anxiety in January 2021.

In the U.S., according to the Harvard Business Review:

- 200 million workdays are lost because of mental health conditions each year
- 60% of employees have never spoken about mental health with anyone at work
- 86% of employees thought company culture should support mental health
- 50% of Millennials, and 75% of Gen Zs, left roles post-pandemic for mental health reasons

Mental Health America reported that one in five American adults will have a diagnosable mental health condition in any year. And 46% of Americans will meet the criteria for a diagnosable mental health condition at some point in their lifetime. As you can see, discussing mental health and wellbeing, and how to incorporate it into people management practices, are essential for the new normal. Very few of us are coming out of the pandemic and lockdown in a better mood. Whether we know it or not, the pandemic has taken a huge toll on our mental health and wellbeing. As we get back to work, it's imperative that organisations are aware of these facts. Staying agile and adaptable is imperative for organisational behaviour and people management practices this side of the pandemic.

Getting mental health and wellbeing right in the workplace isn't about fixing what's not broken. It's understanding that something is remarkably broken, and proactively seeking a way to fix it. The aim going forward should be about getting the best from employees, by being the best employer possible. That's the only credible plan of action for organisations in our new normal. A plan of action built alongside employees will contribute towards reducing the current 57% of days being taken off for mental health issues in just a few years here in the UK. I believe this to be the same on a global scale where depression and anxiety cost $1 trillion a year, according to the World Health Organisation (WHO).

2

The Manager Issue

With getting to know your employees, a skilled line manager is a good place to start. When you look at the origin of the word "manager," it comes from the Latin word "manus," which means "hand." So, it's reasonable to say that a good manager is a "hand," or even a "helping hand" to the people they manage. I found it hilarious that the word "manus" reads so close to the word "anus" which many managers can be. Please excuse my humour, I'm British!

As a manager or an employee, ask yourself how many managers in your organisation fall into the category of an "anus", apologies, I meant "manus" or "helping hand"? Depending on the answer, you'll know if your organisation has an issue with people management. The problem we have today is that managers have become delegators with too many targets, big workloads, and objectives to achieve. This immediately sets them up for failure as the type of manager that's required in the new normal. With no time to be a "hand," they can become disliked and perceived as an overseer rather than a manager. This perception can lead to an "Us vs. Them" culture with managers viewed as the opposition. Once that label is set, nothing can remove it. I'm sure this also rings bells for many readers of this book.

A vicious cycle then develops, creating polarisation between the manager and the team. This can lead to absenteeism, presenteeism, and a toxic workplace and departmental culture. Eventually leading to a lack of respect for the manager and ultimately the employer. When a new member joins the team, they're soon "informed" by the other members of staff about the "manager." This leads to the manager having little chance of a clean slate and fresh start with any new employees, even if they try to make a positive change. This can then result in an "I can't win" mind frame by the manager and, in some cases, managers won't even bother to try. They're convinced that any new member of staff will be poisoned by existing employees eventually, whilst leaving new members of staff feeling they must fit in with the status quo of the team mentality or get sidelined. The atmosphere then becomes abrasive for the manager, and the people they manage, and pernicious for the organisation.

For those who haven't come across the term presenteeism, it's when someone is physically present for work but isn't truly there. Presenteeism is being at work physically, but not mentally, and being unable to be productive. Every one of us has been guilty of presenteeism at some point in our working lives. If you ever showed up for work a bit sick because you didn't want to ask for a day off, did half the work you would normally do, and then went home. You are guilty of presenteeism. Presenteeism linked to poor mental health and wellbeing, however, can last months or even years.

There's a cost to presenteeism, financially for the employer and mentally for the employee. The signs and symptoms of presenteeism can be difficult to identify and evaluate for an untrained manager or HR team, even in small organisations. Presenteeism is less tangible and obvious compared to absenteeism, making it a bigger and more expensive issue for larger organisations. According to

Health Assured in the UK, an independent health and wellbeing provider, the most common causes of presenteeism are:

- Unrealistic employer expectations and time pressures
- No paid sick days
- Lack of loyalty or job insecurity
- Harassment or discrimination for taking sick days
- Larger workloads
- Understaffing

If you're a manager reading this, when did you last check in on a human level with those you manage? When did you last talk to an employee, not because you were asked to do so for some workplace initiative or questionnaire, but because you care? I can almost hear the internal thoughts of managers reading this right now and thinking, "I don't have time for that!" In fact, as a manager, when did someone check in on you? You're also human and an employee. The answers to those questions are a good indicator of where you are as a manager, how you're being managed, and your management team's areas for improvement.

Delegators are taskmasters who are often managed by another taskmaster. A tumbling cascade of "to-do lists," and a mind-numbing blur of back-to-back Teams and Zoom meetings. This is fast becoming the culture of management and organisational behaviour in the new normal. This isn't management, it's digital delegation. This is the culture where tasks are delegated and expected to be completed within a set or reasonable time. In the new normal, we are getting to a place a manager's ability is judged by how efficiently this process is done. Failure at any point in this process could mean a manager is perceived or may fear they'll be perceived, as inadequate by their superiors. To counterbalance this, delegators will crack the whip, working their team harder, and creating resentment and unhappiness in the process. This is the outcome when a manager is a delegator and a taskmaster, or does not possess the skill set required to be a good manager, or is not given the room to be a manager.

Effective managers in the new normal, will be given the freedom to spend 50% of their time managing people and 50% of their time getting tasks done. A 50/50 split is the best practice for people management in the new normal. A supportive manager spending 50% of their time managing people, will always get more out of their team, compared to a manager who spends 100% of their time delegating tasks and demanding results. Having managed a multitude of managers as a CEO and giving them the space required to manage people efficiently, I've witnessed this first-hand.

To get the best from employees, employers will need to listen to their needs and wants. This requires time, space, and, most importantly, that human touch. The best practice to manage people can be through line managers given the space to manage. A manager in a team bigger than five people may require an assistant to oversee tasks while they spend quality time managing people. If there's no support for the manager, managing people becomes an extra workload that will lead to burnout and other issues. Managing people in this 50/50 fashion won't work if the manager is already disliked and not a good, empathetic, and active listener. Organisations need to place certain soft skills at a higher value when recruiting and promoting managers in the new normal.

Interpersonal skills, such as emotional intelligence, empathy, active listening, critical observation, and conflict resolution, should form the foundation of skill requirements when seeking to employ or promote managers. Actively seek those with a natural knack for people to lead as future managers. Managers who are amazing at producing results, but have terrible people skills, should be avoided, they are unable to leverage the true potential of the team they manage. The consequence of this is that the employer never fully utilises their employees' skill set, negatively affecting the ROI for wages paid. A well-run department should never come with the price tag of resentment and unhappiness from staff because of a manager's lack of people skills. Conviviality and being easy to work with is a massively underrated career skill.

In the new normal, managers will need to know some personal aspects of an employee's life. Employers must look beyond the tradition of only being informed on professional aspects and should seek to create a safe space where employees can feel comfortable, sharing information about their personal lives, and developments within their homes. This is a perfect role for someone trained in Mental Health First Aid (MHFA). Both personal and professional circumstances impact a person's mental health continuum. Hybrid working has firmly embedded the workplace within an employee's home. Workplace-based only management practices have had their day. It's time to develop new practices for the hybrid environment. People management practices must be a combination of both professional and personal factors. Ironically, this should've always been the case, as we cannot hang up our mental health along with our jackets and just get on with our working day. Then pick it back up on the way out.

Traditionally, that was what a "professional" was supposed to do. Come to work, be professional and leave. That is far from being a professional. It's a ticking time bomb of mental ill health and burnout. I speak from lived experience when I say that. In 2018, I won one of the most coveted HR and people management awards in the UK. The Investors People Manager of the Year Award. Comedian Russell Kane and Strictly Come Dancing's Alan Dedicoat presented it to me.

Winner! Investors in People Manager of the Year Award 2018

This was one of the highlights of my career, Investors in People looked at the framework and strategy implemented with the 50-strong team I created and established. Due to my people management practices, Investors in People recognised me as a global leader in HR and people management practices and I was given the award. On paper, I was an award-winning and celebrated CEO, featured on the Apprentice, Eden Project, and Business Matters Magazine. The academy was the highest rated and reviewed on Google in the world. For anyone looking at my life externally, it would seem like a tremendous success.

Happy Mum Lilani Perera with Award

Around the same time, and unbeknown to me, my mental health was taking a pounding because of the pressure being a CEO put me under. I spiralled after the Brexit vote in 2016, which led to a significant reduction in students from Europe, representing around 50% of my clients. European students were worried their qualifications wouldn't be valid after Brexit, or if they book courses, they'd have travel issues. Over the next three years, there was a steady decline in European enrolment. Unfortunately, we expanded, doubling our capacity and tripling costs, just before the Brexit vote. This led to a painful three-year process for me as a CEO. I was trying to keep my once bursting-at-the-seams business afloat and was losing the battle. After a decade of extreme success and growth, I liquidated in April 2019.

I wasn't only the CEO, but also the founder, and the loss was personal. I started the business being a silent partner with a good friend and later discovered she was stealing money and had racked up substantial debts. After buying her out, I took full control of the business. I was at university at the time and about to start the third year of a bachelor's degree. I had no choice but to take on the business full-time whilst making a go of it at university. I took calls running in and out of lecture halls and once fell asleep in my suit upright on my bed, trying to juggle a running business as a complete novice and my university work. I had two lives: the university student, and a young pretender businessman. I'd dress casually for university, change in my car and drive to Tottenham Court Road and do the businessman thing. I didn't know what I was doing. I saw the opportunity and figured it out on the way.

When I think back, I'm unsure how I graduated with my bachelor's, completed my MBA the following year, and still got the company out of debt over that period and went on to build a leading brand in a sector I knew nothing about. I used to live in coffee shops and restaurants in and around Warren Street station. I interviewed many of my first members of staff in those same places. Eventually, a friend at university started working for me part-time, helping with the heavy admin the organisation required. This freed up my mind for the entrepreneurial vision needed for the business. She went on to work for me for several years as my operations manager.

One of my most memorable times in business for me was when BBC 1's Apprentice approached us to pitch an online marketing company. They wanted to pitch for us to be a potential client. The Apprentice team was pitching Mark Wright's, Climb Online. We accepted the pitch and offered Mark an initial £24K a year contract. Lord Sugar would have seen the potential of Mark's business idea immediately. It was all televised and it was the first time I'd been on TV. It was an amazing feeling knowing the business I worked so hard to get up and running, made all this possible. All the late nights, hard work, and stress seemed to be worth it. The business was finally putting a smile on my face, rather than giving me problem after problem. The contract we offered was more than likely the reason Mark won the Apprentice that year. Lord Sugar can only confirm that, but I am sure the £24K a year offer wasn't something a well-versed businessman like Lord Sugar would miss seeing the potential in. Mark went on to be Lord Sugar's most successful Apprentice winner and still holds that title in 2022.

Chit Chatting with Apprentice Winner Mark Wright in 2016

Another memorable occasion was when we became finalists at the prestigious British Hairdressing Awards for the Afro Hairdresser of the Year and Avant Garde Hairdresser of the Year Award categories in 2016.

In 2018, we went to Sri Lanka to do a shoot for Colombo Fashion Week in collaboration with Stefan Joachim and Nick Saglimbeni. The photoshoot took place in a beautiful derelict British colonial post office in Colombo.

**Me, Nick Saglimbeni, and Stefan Joachim with
Staff from the London Makeup School**

Nick working on set In Sri Lanka

This period of my life was special, and I think back to it in amazement and nostalgia. The academy was a shining beacon of what hard work, persistence, dedication, and not taking no for an answer can achieve. In hindsight, I realised the reason this was a special time was because of the things the academy achieved. Those achievements were only made possible by the people and personalities involved and how they were managed. It's what inspired me to write this book and losing it wasn't easy for me by any means. Two days after I liquidated, my daughter told me I was going to be a grandad. That entire period of my life was overwhelming. I dealt with it in the same fashion I had always dealt with my struggles in life. I brushed myself off and got on with it. That time, however, my mental health threw the towel in.

I remember a couple of my staff and friends checked in on me briefly, shortly after the liquidation. Besides that, I was on my own, dealing with losing over a decade of my life's work. Now that I'm more aware mentally, I realise the importance of family and a supportive community for a person going through the trauma of any major loss.

Oddly, it was one of my nephews, Tariq Perera, and one of the youngest in my family that took the time to come see me shortly afterwards. I didn't see the importance of his visit, even annoyed he had taken time out of his day to come and check in on me. In hindsight, I realised he was displaying a trait of empathy and awareness my family and I critically lack. As for the rest of my family and friends, I gathered they viewed it as more in line with losing a job, which is quite different. My good friend and mentor, Graham Shapiro, also came to see me shortly after the liquidation. As a successful and award-winning businessperson, Graham was one of the very few people in my life that truly understood what I was experiencing. As the saying goes, it's lonely at the top, and being a CEO can be an extremely lonely place, especially when problems arise.

I watched an interview with Steven Bartlett, who said all CEOs should be in therapy. I couldn't agree with him more. Therefore, whenever I consult or train organisations, I always ask if the person booking the training (usually the HR or learning and development manager) will be taking the training. Along with the CEO and everyone in the higher level of management, because they must, due to the pressure of their roles.

Getting Ready for British Hairdressing Awards

Preparing for Our Annual General Meeting!

Shortly after the liquidation, I was diagnosed with mixed depression and anxiety disorder. I was written off work for over a year to recover. I went from a high-flying, highly paid CEO, who created two well-known brands and managed a team of fifty staff, to a person who struggled to put an email together. I didn't have the knowledge or understanding of how my mental health worked, or how to mentally look after myself. It took fourteen months to reach a mental state where I could function at my normal level.

The irony was, I'd spent the previous three years building an award winning HR and wellbeing framework that I insisted my staff be a part of, yet I didn't think at any stage it was important to apply to myself. This is a mistake many CEOs and senior managers make. Many feel they are above this type of learning. I was always under the impression that mental health issues were for weak people, and I was a strong person, so no need to worry about it. If I'd known some of the most basic knowledge taught in MHFA, such as knowledge around the mental health continuum, or that one in four people in the UK will develop a diagnosable mental health condition in any year, or that my ethnicity makes me three times more likely to develop a mental health issue in the UK, things may have been different. Had I possessed some basic mental health awareness, or had some training, the mental illness I developed, and everything that came with it, could've been avoided.

During that period, a weekend of drinking always followed a stressful or hectic week. Whether it was a good or a bad week, it led to drinking. This is a lifestyle many people in the UK live. We call it culture, but in fact, it's coping. That's why around 75% of people with a diagnosable mental illness receive no treatment. They're literally walking around unaware they've developed a diagnosable mental health condition and require professional help.

My mental health condition could've cost me my life, as it does for over five thousand people every year in the UK. If it did, I wouldn't be here doing what I'm doing today. I've trained hundreds of people in MHFA and gone through the difficult, life-changing process of loss and recovery. I wouldn't have met my granddaughter Shaiya, who is my world. I wouldn't be engaged with my wedding planned for 2023. I wouldn't have created my organisation, Mental Health and Life and you wouldn't be reading this book.

In June 2020, I stopped a nineteen-year-old boy in Pembrokeshire Wales from killing himself (my greatest achievement to date), he randomly called my organisation in desperation as he was preparing to take his own life. After doing mental health first aid with him, I got the police and the ambulance to assist him. He phoned me six weeks later to thank me for saving his life. I eventually hope to open UK's first mental health first aid hotline, under his name.

All of this happened in the space of three short years. Just like nobody needs to die from a broken finger or a broken arm, nobody needs to die from a mental health condition. There are infinite reasons to live, and not just to live, but to live happy, healthy, and well. There's a vast difference between the two. I must mention Dr Rollinson from the Vauxhall Health Centre in Liverpool, who showed me the care and attention I deserved to help my recovery. Something we've tragically lost in our GP practices in the UK. My doctor at Glen Road Medical Centre in Plaistow told me he can only deal with one issue at a time. He asked me what my most pressing issue was, I told him I was struggling to sleep. He then prescribed me with enough sleeping tablets that I could have used to killed myself with, while I was severely depressed, and practically threw me out of his room. This was one of the main reasons I left London, and an experience replicated up and down the country in GP practices. We seem to have lost the "care" in healthcare.

I recently learned most GPs in the UK have no mental health or MHFA training. This is likely why people with a dual diagnosis (a person with both a mental disorder and an alcohol or drug problem) are almost always prescribed medication by their GP. A practice that needs to be looked at urgently by the healthcare sector. Medication combined with mental ill health and substance misuse can be lethal. I realised London as a city, and everything that comes with it, was a major risk factor for my mental health. Therefore, I left and moved to Liverpool where I've come across some of the nicest people I have ever met in the UK. I live on a "Blue" road, and Everton has become my adopted second team. West Ham United, of course, being my actual team!

As I learned more about mental health, I realised the pressure as a CEO that led to my diagnosis was only the straw that broke the camel's back. My therapist explained I had experienced severe trauma since childhood. He informed me that from the ages of 6–40, in his words, my trauma was "substantially more than the average person." Some traumas I hadn't considered to be traumas, but had a major impact on my mental health, wellbeing, and my character. Through therapy, I realised I hadn't checked in on myself for four decades. The psychological impact of the trauma I carried around had affected every aspect of my life. Eventually, at forty years old, it all came home to roost.

When I got better, I asked myself what do I want to do as a forty-plus man? The first thing I decided was that I'd never put myself under such abnormal pressure in any environment in my life, personal or professional. As I investigated mental health, I realised MHFA was at the frontline for prevention and self-care. I felt deep inside that everything that happened, led me to a certain place in my life. I left the corporate world and followed my heart, not my ego, my vanity, my bank balance, or the indoctrinated view of success. I launched my organisation Mental Health and Life to prevent anyone else from going through what I had. The more I educated myself on mental health, the more I understood that everything that happened to me was preventable, highlighting the importance of my current work.

My experience of mental ill health is a good example of why people management practices must be a hybrid of both professional and personal factors. The whole "be a professional" approach to managing people is defunct. In the new normal, it's more of a "be a human" approach that must be taken. We take our mental health everywhere with us. It affects everything we do and all aspects of our lives. Forward-thinking employers and managers in the new normal will understand this. The new normal has finally given us an immense opportunity to get things right in the workplace.

The question then becomes, how do organisations do that?

One of the most important things to know as an employer and manager is the mental health continuum

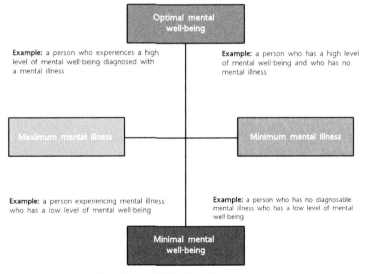

The Mental Health Continuum

The mental health continuum displays how our mental health is fluid and changes over time. We can move around the continuum yearly, monthly, or even weekly, depending on what life throws at us. We all must appreciate that our mental health is fluid and constantly changing. We all exist somewhere in one of the four quadrants on the continuum. As a reader, ask yourself where you are right now on the continuum. Remember to be honest with yourself. If you're not in the top right-hand quadrant, getting help is essential.

Before my diagnosis, I was a person who thought mental illness was something I wouldn't have to worry about. There are many people in the world, and within organisations, that think this way. The mental health continuum helps us acknowledge if we're living, mental ill health is likely. What is guaranteed with a person's mental health is that they'll never stay in one quadrant of the continuum throughout their lifetime. This is life's dark humour of constantly kicking us down to see if we'll get back up. No one is exempt from the fluidity in their mental health and the factors that impact movement around the continuum.

The risk factors that can affect a person's mental health are:

- Discrimination and Stigma
- Poverty or homelessness
- Social isolation or loneliness
- Drug or alcohol abuse
- Being a long-term carer
- Abuse, trauma or neglect
- Domestic violence
- Unemployment or losing a job
- Severe long-term stress
- Military combat and severe trauma an adult

- Physical illnesses
- Death of a loved one

*This is not an exhaustive list

Looking at these risk factors, it's impossible for any person not to be affected. These risk factors impact a person from childhood onward. The pandemic threw fuel on the fire and exacerbated these risk factors for millions of people. People lost their jobs, leading to financial troubles, and domestic abuse skyrocketed. In Liverpool, domestic violence killed four women during the lockdown over one weekend. One street over from where I live, a woman was discovered dead in her front room from an alcohol and drug overdose. Almost everyone lost a loved one or someone they know lost a loved one. The death toll is still rising at the time of writing this book, around 200 people a day. I lost my father during the pandemic; we couldn't visit him during the two weeks he spent in the hospital. It was only when he was dying the hospital allowed family to visit, and by the time I got from Liverpool to London, he had died. These traumatic experiences were repeated UK-wide by millions of people during the pandemic. Take a minute to look at the risk factors and ask yourself how many have affected your life since childhood.

Understanding the mental health continuum and risk factors for mental health is vital for managers and employers. Every time someone moves quadrant, the level of support required from an employer or manager changes. An employer can be sure when a person does move quadrant, it will affect the way they live their lives and how they work. This understanding is crucial since one in four people will develop a diagnosable mental health issue in any year. Once an employer or manager understands the continuum, they can better manage people and themselves.

This dismantles the age-old notion that if an employee performs well at a certain part of the year, then poorly in another part of the year. They've lost interest, don't care, or have given up. It may have nothing to do with those negative conclusions. We are all preprogramed to be negative, it's an ancient defence mechanism, so jumping to negative conclusions both in life and work are common. Therefore, it could simply be, that the employee has moved a quadrant on their continuum because of a life event. The impact of that movement is the reason their performance at work declined. Without the knowledge of the continuum, which most managers worldwide lack, it's easy to jump to such conclusions. That type of thinking creates a cycle of polarisation between the employer and employee, when the employee needs extra support.

If you're a manager or an employee, were you aware of the mental health continuum? If not, how has that affected your management style or working life?

In the new normal we are building; employees must stop convincing themselves that the changes that need to be had in the workplace, are too big. As an employee, which includes managers, it's imperative to keep pushing the agenda on mental health and better management practices. It is a two-way street, and it will make your working life that much better.

Below is a list of comments I've gathered during my courses when I've asked why essential information that can ease the working day and improve operational functions, isn't persistently highlighted and worked towards:

- I don't want to be a troublemaker
- I'll ignore this, it's above my pay grade
- There's too much hierarchy and red tape for such a change to occur

- They don't listen, anyway; it goes up and vanishes
- I'm not a manager
- Our manager listens and does nothing
- My manager wouldn't care
- The company is too big to consider such a change
- Decisions are made abroad or at another head office
- I just want my pay cheque; they should know what's good for them
- It's just the way things are
- They don't care about all this stuff

I could go on, and I'm sure this list rings bells at your workplace, too. I hear these comments all the time during my MHFA training courses and when consulting. Most people agree during the training course that certain changes would make things better for everyone in the organisation. Bizarrely, the agenda isn't pushed, or employees feel powerless to push it. That seems to be the reality in a lot of organisations, both small and large. I've trained and spoken with many organisations and their employees over the last three years. During that time, the working world transitioned from the old normal to the new normal. The biggest change to affect the working world and work-life balance in recent history. Over this period, my clients have ranged from CEOs to office juniors, and the organisations have ranged from small to medium enterprises (SMEs) to multinational Public Limited Companies (PLCs). A theme I've discovered is that no matter who they are, when dealing with feedback from their staff, many seem stuck in a rut, like a deer caught in the headlights.

Some organisations go as far as putting processes in place to receive feedback. Actioning the feedback, however, is out of their reach. That inaction in the new normal will minimise productivity and performance, as it did in the old normal. Asking for feedback and not doing anything about it is regressive and decreases staff morale. Organisations are better off not asking for feedback if they can't act on what pops up. When staff view feedback as a tick-box exercise leading to nothing, they'll engage less with workplace initiatives and changes. Companies who did well pre-pandemic probably don't realise they could've done a lot better if this inaction didn't exist. The best practice for engagement prior to asking for feedback is to first check in on employees' mental health and wellbeing. This will ensure the quality of the data; all workplace improvements start with the human.

In our new normal, employers and managers must be mentally literate. One in four adults in the UK will experience at least one "diagnosable" mental health issue in any year. In the U.S., it's one in five. The reason I've used quotation marks on "diagnosable" is that most people won't get a diagnosis because of the stigma attached to mental ill health. This creates issues for both the employer and the employee. These statistics show employers must make space for mental health issues at work. People cannot hang their mental health up with their jackets and get on with work. They are humans, not robots. There are other considerations. The Guardian, in January 2021, reported that over six million people are on anti-depressants in the UK, the highest figure on record.

If you're an employer, CEO, or manager reading this book right now,

- Are you aware of how many of your employees are on anti-depressants?
- Are you aware of how many of your employees have mental health conditions this side of the pandemic?
- If you are, have you conversed with them so you can give them the workplace support they require?

The answers to these questions will spell out your areas of improvement within your job role and responsibility.

Now, let's consider why it's crucial for an organisation to be mentally literate and why it's essential to have a robust and well-developed support system in place for mental health at work.

Here are some factors that affect mental health in the workplace:

- Dangerous and poor physical working environments
- Traumatic experiences (Think blue light services)
- Unmanageable workloads, long hours and job pressure
- Lack of control over work and poor management
- Lack of autonomy and involvement in organisational change
- Inadequate pay, poor reward and recognition processes
- Not feeling "seen" at work
- Bullying, mental health stigma and bad relationship with peers
- Feeling expendable

*This is not an exhaustive list

These factors aren't exhaustive, and many other factors come into play depending on the job, role, and sector. This list gives a general idea of the most common factors affecting mental health within the workplace. When looking at this list, it can seem overwhelming for an organisation to deal with. A mountain too big to climb, yet organisations created this monster, and it will be organisations that must change things for the better, bringing that monster to heel. We've reached a time in history when not addressing mental health in the workplace isn't an option. The time for sweeping it under the rug and pretending it's not there is over. Change is possible and organisations need not panic, as the change doesn't need to happen overnight, it can happen over time. One of the most important and impactful processes that an organisation can implement to rectify oversights of the past, is quite a small and cost-efficient step.

Best practice for organisations to address mental health in the workplace and create a solid foundation for any wellbeing framework is through MHFA training. True mental health literacy is about empowering people to look after themselves and those around them. This is the essence of MHFA training. No matter how much space and process an organisation provides for mental health, if employees don't have mental health awareness and understand the benefits of that awareness, the process becomes futile, and many employees naturally disengage. Employers and managers reading this may think "that sounds a bit like our EAP." I hope it does, as we then agree that engagement is a by-product of awareness. Almost all the things an individual can do for good mental health lie in their own hands and actions unless it's genetically linked. I always tell my learners in my courses, "You are the CEO of your life." If you owned a business, would you decide to run your business into the ground daily? No? So why do we do it with our health?

When a person needs a third party to get involved with their mental health, it's usually because they've made continuous bad decisions whether knowingly, or unknowingly regarding their mental health. Most people who develop mental health issues are guilty of these bad decisions, outside of those with certain personality disorders and genetically linked conditions. Once organisations understand this, they can educate and empower employees to look after and support themselves as individuals. There's no generic solution to wellbeing as we've discovered from pre-pandemic data. Empowering employees to look after themselves via MHFA training is an easy step, yet it will create monumental outcomes for mental health at work if an organisation acts on the training. When an organisation empowers employees in this way, half of addressing mental health at work is complete, believe it or not. The remaining 50% takes a lot more effort and will be a continuous work in progress.

MHFA training is the foundation of what organisations in the new normal will require to build any fit-for-purpose wellbeing framework. It's the first step towards awareness and literacy. As we move forward into 2022 and beyond, and the working world moves on globally, the consequences of what happened to us during the lockdown will unravel. Many people will enter the new normal with lower levels of wellbeing. Many of us will have undiagnosed, or diagnosed, mental health conditions.

MHFA training is important as the average person doesn't understand how to deal with themselves or others when it comes to mental health. People who, without a second thought, would call their doctor or go to the hospital for a physical health issue, suddenly become their own experts in mental health, leading to disastrous consequences lasting years. What I've discovered in delivering training is that people think they're literate regarding their mental health and wellbeing. Many, however, are not.

Mental ill health isn't a physical injury, so many feel it doesn't require the same level of priority. Thus, it's viewed as something that can be dealt with later. Many people feel they know how mental health works and what needs to be done to stay healthy. What I've discovered through my training is the opposite. Nearly everyone who attends my courses leave surprised at their lack of knowledge of mental health. Most people finish their training, realising just how proactive they can, and need to be, when it comes to looking after their mental health. There's also a misconception about MHFA training because of the words "first aid." Many people see MHFA training as something you do to help someone else, like First Aid at Work. As with First Aid at Work, what you learn in a mental health first aid course you can apply to yourself. In fact, with MHFA training, I'd say it applies to yourself first and foremost. The training is a manual for life, and essential learning for every single person in the UK and worldwide.

3

Benefits of Mental Health First Aid Training

Feedback from my MHFA courses is almost always along the lines of how learners didn't know, just how much they can do for themselves. How the course has changed their lives. If you don't believe me, read my Google reviews or my LinkedIn recommendations. Mental health seems to be the only part of our "health" that people assume they're qualified to deal with, without any formal education. The opposite of how most people deal with their physical health. MHFA training levels the playing field, MHFA courses equip the everyday person with the skills to address the gaping void between someone becoming unwell and getting the help they need.

People ignore their mental health as it's not something we can see, such as being overweight or having an injury. They then develop mental health issues, and substance misuse issues and, in the worst case, die by suicide before they get help. People dealing with mental health this way aren't only unfair to themselves, but also to those around them. People who ignore their mental health needs expect other people to do the same and "just get on with it," adding to the stigma around mental ill health. Unfortunately, we all work differently, with different levels of coping and resilience. For a person who cannot just get on with it, struggling can bring feelings of guilt. This approach to mental health, both in society and within organisations, is unacceptable and unfair!

Mental health has two stigmas: social and self-stigma. Social stigma, sometimes called public stigma, is the negative stereotypes about a person experiencing a mental health condition that singles that person out and defines them according to their condition. This can lead to the person not reaching out for help. Social stigma is associated with discrimination and breaches anti-discrimination laws in the UK. Self-stigma occurs when a person with a mental health condition internalises these negative stereotypes, leading to a person undergoing many negative consequences. Stigma is vicious, both in the workplace and in life.

MHFA courses are training programs for the everyday person to help someone developing or experiencing a mental health issue. It trains a person to have a supportive conversation and how to signpost to professional help. It trains people on how to look after their own mental health and wellbeing. With MHFA training and its application, it's the same as when you're told to put on your oxygen mask before helping others on a plane in an emergency. This is the same for being a mental health first aider. You must ensure you're in a place of good health and wellbeing before you can help others. A point brilliantly articulated by my instructor, Sean Liddell, when I first trained as an MHFA.

**Training to be a Mental Health First Aider with
MHFA England Instructor Sean Liddell**

The self-application and self-empowerment the training provides are a godsend to employers. The training not only teaches employees to keep a watchful eye on their colleagues, but to keep a watchful eye on themselves. This mental health autonomy and literacy in employees not only makes an organisation's corporate social responsibility sparkle, but it also takes away a huge burden in trying to figure out what's best for employees with their wellbeing and how they're managed. Empowerment should always be the first step for mental health literacy in the workplace.

MHFA also prevents organisations from barking up the wrong tree with generic, off-the-shelf solutions to wellbeing. Instead, with MHFA training, the organisation isn't passing the buck. The training makes it so that organisations can identify and acknowledge the needs of their employees whilst empowering them to look after their own wellbeing. The training produces specific data on employee needs and wants while generating ideas for operational processes. The data is nothing short of gold dust for employers. It's the best way to build a fit-for-purpose wellbeing framework, department by department, that is unique to an organisation and their employees.

Giving employees the power to look after themselves in return for data that is unique is true data no book, expert, or consultant can provide. Perhaps they can provide it for a cost, but why would employers want that overhead when they can easily have a constant flow of invaluable data on people management and wellbeing at a fraction of the cost? The data can then be leveraged by creating simple and effective communication channels within the organisation where this data is actively mined in a reasonable time and changes implemented as and when they can be. What employers will find is that even small changes that occur due to staff feedback from MHFA training can lift morale, instantly affecting the culture of the workplace positively. There's no better way for an employer to say we care about you as a person, than through MHFA training.

Employers will find, as I've discovered through delivering courses, that some things employees require are small, usually related to physical stressors. For example, having more water stations or plants in the office, or fixing a creaking chair. One organisation I trained let staff bring in their own plants to the office! The reduction of these quick-fix stressors can be implemented quickly and with minimal fuss or major toll on finances. It's a small thing for the employer but a big thing for employees. It can make the staff feel seen, heard, and appreciated; a contrivance some workplaces have lost. These simple changes give an organisation breathing space with changes that require more time to implement, yet let employees know they've been heard. I can't overstate that in the new normal, organisations genuinely need to focus on the needs and wants of their most valuable assets, their employees!

Incorporation of MHFA courses is essential for people management practices in the new normal. Once people realise how their mental health works, and how to look after it, and how to watch for signs of mental ill health in themselves and others. It brings a long-lost human element into HR and people management. MHFA training brings about an understanding that everyone in the hierarchy at work is human. This human connection is essential for good employee relations. Once employees perceive their colleagues are going through the same troubles and strife on a human level, employees will naturally interact in a more empathetic and humane manner. This human element naturally connects to the human nature and goodness we all have within us, thus helping us to deal with each other in a gentler way.

The future of people management is to manage people like they're your friends and family by creating a family feel to management and developing a work environment nothing short of an extended family. Let's call it "the work family." Why would we not? Many of us spend more time at work than with our families. By default, does that not make colleagues a part of an extended family? Who made the rules to keep colleagues at an arm's length and maintain professional boundaries? Maybe it had its positives in a bygone era, but it has no a place in the new normal. When we reconsider management in this way, we automatically get to know people better, and on a human level. This leads to a more holistic way of thinking in management that considers all aspects of a person's life. If you think about it, is it even possible to truly manage a person without such an approach? Yes, organisations, managers, and HR departments might have to put some work in, but won't it be worth it?

What we know for sure, is that we cannot continue on as we are, when it comes to managing people.

In 2018, a few months before I won the Manager of the Year Award, I attended a course at the Eden Project in Cornwall called Hot House: Nature of Leadership programme. I'd become disillusioned with the current mantra of leadership and who I was as a leader. I felt like I needed CPD as managing staff and being a CEO was a constant work in progress. As I looked online for a good leadership development programme, I found nothing on the market that appealed to me. Nothing seemed to match what I felt as a CEO and as a person. A lot of the leadership learning available I felt I covered during my MBA. I was searching for something outside the status quo, a programme not overly focused on company growth and status, rather inner growth as a person. It was then I stumbled on the course at the Eden Project, described as a programme designed for emerging leaders wanting to be a force for good via their businesses and communities. It was exactly what I was searching for, a complete digital detox based in nature, self-reflection and doing some good in the world as a business leader.

**The Hot House: Nature of Leadership programme -
Group Activities at a Beach in Cornwall**

Feeling, Touching, and Immersing in Nature

Some Souvenirs to Take Home

I attended the course in April 2018, and it was a life-changing and reflective experience leading to two major developments within my organisation. I decided that, in my heart of hearts, I couldn't live at peace knowing how much animal cruelty is involved in the beauty industry.

As a business owner who spent hundreds of thousands on animal-tested products each year, I knew my organisation was a major contributor to that cruelty. I fell out of love with my business for the first time. As I contemplated how ugly the beauty industry was, I remembered that, ever since I was a kid, my only true passion was animals. I remember running home from school to watch the Really Wild Show with Terry Nutkins, Michaela Strachan, and Chris Packham. Outside of my parents, I don't have many heroes. I'm hard to impress. There's Tupac, Tesla, Turing, Attenborough and Mandela, that's about it. Words like "genius," "brilliant," and "influential" are thrown around willy-nilly these days, an insult to those who truly are.

From a young age, David Attenborough was one of my heroes and one that is still alive. Even at forty-four, I still hang on every word he says exactly as I did as a child. Attenborough captured my mind as he'd done with millions. I remember my first day at an infant school in the UK when I couldn't speak or read English. My teacher picked me out an animal book and showed me a picture of a Cheetah. I was instantly hooked. Nature programs and the likes of Terry Nutkins and David Attenborough only added to my love of the natural world. Because of this influence, I had fantasised about going back to my country of birth and getting involved in elephant, sloth bear, and leopard conservation. That's still my eventual goal for the latter stages of my life. I remember listening intently as my parents would speak about the human-elephant conflict in Sri Lanka as a kid and feeling angry at the humans. My parents were always on the elephants' side.

During the course, I pondered how I grew up to own a business in an industry that tortured and maimed billions of animals every year. Had I sold my soul to an industry without even realising it, or was there another reason I was there? I needed to step back and re-evaluate what my life had become. I decided at the Eden Project I would make a dramatic change in my business. A change no one in the industry dared to do or, more than likely, even considered at the time. It would mean turning our backs on the biggest brands in the industry, our main suppliers and partnerships. I decided the academy would transition to being 100% cruelty-free. This decision, however, wasn't mine to make. I wasn't the industry professional. Ultimately, the yes or no would come from the academy managers. They held the knowledge of the brands we needed for the transition. That was the first development.

**Fun in the Mediterranean Biome with
Course Facilitator Mike Smith**

The second development was the realisation that I was guilty of keeping my staff at an arm's length. I'd done this on purpose for a decade. I thought that was how professional boundaries between employees, and myself as the business owner and CEO, were supposed to be. My staff only knew me as Richie the boss, but that was only a small part of me. I had staff who worked for me for over a decade, who had started single, found partners, had kids, and bought homes while being my employee. Yet I hardly knew these people outside of work. I asked myself, why didn't I know more about these people's lives?

One activity in the course was about crossing thresholds with people as a leader. Getting to know my staff better was a threshold I had to cross to be a better leader. As a leader, it was important that I knew more about their personal lives. One facilitator asked if I had ever invited my staff into my home, as thresholds are also physical. I realised besides two members of staff who were friends from university and a few managers who came to my house because of a fire in the building; I hadn't let my team cross the threshold into my home. I remember sitting there thinking how odd it was and why I hadn't considered it before. When I got back to London, I killed two birds with one stone. I invited some of my management team to my home to break the news about the cruelty-free transition and threw a party to celebrate on my roof terrace!

My management Team's First Time in my Home

When the team came to my home, I immediately noticed how natural it felt, like a bunch of good friends coming over. I knew them. It felt nice to let them know I was a human, too. I always played the traditional role of a CEO, taking on all issues and problems at work, trying to be strong and together all the time. My staff being in my home felt like I was showing them I am also a human, with hopes, dreams, and fears, just like everyone else. Look, I even have a bed and require sleep, and have hobbies and interests outside of running a company. I have a personality outside of "boss mode." I have a certain taste in music and in the way I decorate my home.

I realised inviting my staff into my home helped them understand me better. The good news was that both academy managers confirmed the transition to cruelty-free was possible. It would take some planning and time, but it was doable. As you'll gather by the timeline of these events, we never got to see the academy transition into the only cruelty-free academy in the world. Brexit put a stop to that, and we liquidated a year later. People and organisations may die, but an idea lives forever. Another CEO in the sector may read this and be inspired to do the same, or even approach me with a plan. I welcome it, it's unfinished business for me.

As CEOs, decision-makers, and managers, it's vital to cross thresholds in the new normal. We need to connect with our employees who are essentially an extended family and see them in that light. Together, we're not only stronger, but more efficient. Together we have the power to change the working world for the better. That's not an overstatement. If you look at some of the biggest organisations in the world, they seem to be a gift and curse for humanity. The time has come to make decisions on the side of the gift rather than the curse. The biggest corporations in the world have more money, power, and influence than many governments in the world. Why not use that influence to secure a better future for us all? If anyone will change the world, it will be big business. A time to make that decision has come, an opportune moment, as they say. The question is, what will big businesses do with it? Will they carry on stashing money they won't get around to spending? Or will they spend that money in the right way and be the change the world is so desperate for?

The new normal is the tipping point for big businesses to do the right thing. If they do, everyone else will follow suit, including governments. In the new normal, this vision is the future if ambitions such as performance, culture, growth, profitability, retaining talent, saving the planet, corporate social responsibility, and productivity are salient for organisations. Organisations that adopt this thinking and culture won't only see issues such as absenteeism and presenteeism, burnout and staff turnover decline, all of which have a positive impact on workplace culture, wellbeing, and the bottom line. They'll also inadvertently make an invaluable social and societal impact. Organisations in the new normal have this duty of care when considering our planet dying, and mental health issues costing billions globally.

Humans are creatures of their environment and of habit, so much so that our accents, words, and behaviours change even if we travel across the same city. This is true in London, where you'll see differences in dialect and even accents as you go from East, West, North, or South London. Where I live in Liverpool, Manchester is only a forty-minute drive, yet Scousers and Mancunians are different in their mannerisms and accents. Why bring this up? Well, as I've said, humans are creatures of their environment and habit. We live in a world where our most active hours, our main habitat and environment, are the workplace. We spend more time at work or working than with our families. When an organisation gets wellbeing right in the workplace, creating true, specific, supportive, and nurturing processes to manage, train, and empower employees; it will naturally transition into people's personal and social lives, creating a much healthier society. It will affect how we deal with our children, our peers, our social circles, and ourselves. It has the potential to lift millions out of mental ill health, halt the global mental health pandemic, and increase wellbeing exponentially. That's powerful. Every organisation has the power to change the status quo for the better, for employees and themselves.

As we proceed post-pandemic, people will go back to the office or remain working from home. Both have unique sets of mental health challenges that must be addressed. There's a mountain of evidence directly linking how a mentally healthy workforce affects an organisation's bottom line, growth, and culture. There's no need to push that agenda. Organisations either get it, or they don't. The data available has made the decision to prioritise and nurture workplace mental health for us. With this knowledge we have on mental health and wellbeing, is it possible for us as humans, to get vaccinated and just get back to work? Would that be humanely possible?

Therefore, we're presented with a paramount decision regarding the world of work. What we decide determines not only the time it will take economies to bounce back, but also how we work for generations to come. We can make a huge change for the better, and it starts with us humans. How we address workplace mental health and wellbeing now will be the deciding factor of where we'll be in the next decade. The decisions we make now will personally, professionally, and financially determine the state of the economy and wellbeing worldwide. Any organisation undertaking MHFA aid training will comply with several pieces of legislation surrounding workplace health. They'll benefit from reduced absence and staff turnover, enhance their reputation, improve teamwork and productivity, and establish morale at higher levels. This will make that organisation more attractive to new talent, with a positive mental health culture becoming a priority for many post-pandemic.

It helps create a culture that engages with how younger millennials and the incoming workforce of Gen Zs think. They'll avoid organisations that don't put wellbeing first. MHFA training in the workplace can help an organisation create a framework for wellbeing alongside their employees; creating a culture of inclusivity where both people and profit flourish. You cannot truly have one without the other, future-proofing an organisation via sustainability and a culture that sets a new benchmark for corporate social responsibility.

The future of work is where all stakeholders in a business are treated with the same respect and relevance as shareholders and customers. The future of work is where there is no "Us Vs. Them" struggle between employer and employee. A crisis that's got worse over the last two decades and increased exponentially over the last five years. The future of work isn't paying minimum wage with zero benefits while working longer hours, with the organisation being the only side benefitting from the deal. Those days are ending. The new normal is something we're creating right now, and we're the architects of our future.

The future of work is where an organisation is more of a family working together for a mutually beneficial purpose. Organisations need to act to find that happy place for both employer and employee and become the architects of a better working world. This is the opportune moment as a shift has begun. It's coming at organisations like a freight train. Over the next decade, there will be two types of organisations, organisations that recognised the need for change and adapted, and organisations who didn't and got hit by the train!

4

The Great Resignation

Call it what you want: the great resignation, the big quit, the great attrition, or the big shuffle. It's the other pandemic of current times with people quitting their jobs by the millions. It is happening and, when retention issues, staff, and skills shortages become problematic for organisations, the outcome is always detrimental. This shift in the workforce's thinking has come about for several reasons. It is the freight train coming at employers full speed. It's time for organisations to pay attention and not mistake the great resignation as a passing trend. The great resignation is the ever-evolving mindset of the current global workforce. The age of "bullshit jobs" is rapidly ending, and that's good news for people and inadvertently, for businesses.

The pandemic was a spiritual awakening for millions of workers. It's come with the realisation that workers do have power over their working conditions. Employees realise globally, that work isn't a dictatorship governed and controlled by the employer, solely for the benefit of shareholders and business owners. Organisations that were built on job misery and time theft, or billionaire owners who blast off on spaceships to stroke their egos and show the world how wonderful they are, are now the most out-of-touch business leaders in the world. Yet they still own some of the biggest corporations on the planet. How much longer will such business models and ethics be sustainable, will be answered soon.

I'm not being one-sided when I make this point. If you take a handful of billionaires and look at their philanthropy and charity work, some of it is astounding. If I was one of them, I'd imagine the world is filled with "haters," people who can't or don't want to see all the good I do in the world. The fact is, everyone can see it. What these billionaires don't seem to appreciate is that money made from "bullshit jobs" will never justify their philanthropy. They're in total denial of that fact and have forgotten the first rule of charity: it begins at home and, in their case, it begins with their employees. Until these billionaires realise this, their names will always leave a foul taste in a person's mouth. They'll continue to be hated by their workforce and disliked by the general population. The current situation with some of the biggest corporations in the world and their owners reminds me of the song by Bob Marley called "So Much Trouble in the World," where he sings:

> "You see men sailing on their ego trip
> Blast off on their spaceship
> Million miles from reality
> No care for you, no care for me."

The tide is turning for this business set-up and model. I'm one of the growing trend of consumers that aggressively refuses to shop with certain online retailers and purchase from billionaire-owned companies. Rain, sleet, hail, or snow, I'll walk down the road and get what I need from a local business. I've found that local businesses are cheaper for many items, and I get fresh air and exercise, a win-win for me. The customer ultimately has all the power and the money. We can run the world with our wallets. If an organisation falls below the basic standard in the treatment of their employees, we can simply stop consuming from them while other people choose not to be employed by them. It's that easy, and the time has come to set aside our conveniences and do what's right.

The true power of change can be found in people's wallets. It's essential in the new normal that we exercise that power for a better deal at work for all. Lack of job dignity may be a part of the huge shift towards union membership, both in the UK and the U.S., over the pandemic. According to the U.S. Labour Statistics, in December 2020 the global employee talent shortage amounted to a shortage of 40 million skilled workers worldwide, leading to potential losses of $8.4 trillion in revenue for businesses. They warned that the great resignation has the power to blindside companies.

Microsoft's global survey backed the finding with their own study, which found that 41% of the global workforce considered leaving their employer in 2021. Microsoft reported that 37% of the global workforce says their employers are asking too much of them during a pandemic. Employees feel disconnected from their employer with out-of-touch business leaders saying they're "thriving right now," whilst Gen Zs, women, and frontline workers reported struggling more than ever. Microsoft reported that leaders are out of touch with employees and need a wake-up call. The survey also found in organisations where productivity was the same or higher during 2021, was had at a human cost.

One in five global survey respondents said their employers don't care about their work-life balance, 50% feel overworked, 39% feel exhausted, and the digital intensity of workers' days has increased substantially after shifting to hybrid working. Gallup, an American analytics and advisory company based in Washington, D.C. picked up on the overworking of employees back in 2014. They revealed that people in the U.S. worked an average of 47 hours a week, with 18% working over 60 hours a week. They found that regardless of a "living to work" type of life, full-time minimum wage employees still couldn't afford an apartment in any U.S. state without taking on a second job.

If your organisation shifted to hybrid working, consider how this is being managed. Organisations have a duty of care for their employees, whether they're working from home or the office. That duty of care has equal standing in both environments. Organisations shouldn't get complacent with health, safety, and people management within employees' homes. Any employer or manager assuming staff working from home will automatically be fine, because they are in their home, are setting themselves up for some major legal issues. Working from home must be managed effectively, and it needs to be managed now, not later. I've come across a lot of organisations relieved at the lack of people management required since hybrid working came into play. Hybrid working creates new management challenges which organisations aren't prepared for or even aware of. Hybrid working hasn't eased the labour of people management. In fact, it's created new challenges that point toward the need for even more attention towards staff.

Organisations that get complacent with hybrid working will unnecessarily create issues for themselves. Hybrid working had the biggest impact on home life we've ever experienced, naturally affecting health and safety, performance, and wellbeing. As an employer or manager, you must ask how your organisation is looking at that human aspect and addressing the impact within the home environment, A simple example can be found in the manner employees take breaks. Taking breaks correctly is essential, not only for your wellbeing but also for your engagement and performance at work.

If you're an employee that doesn't take breaks correctly, works through your lunch, eats at your desk, and emails colleagues after working hours, you're a bad employee. If you're a manager who does the same, you're not a good manager. Employees who take their breaks correctly and disconnect from work are more engaged, productive, and perform better than those who don't. An employer who doesn't educate and manage such behaviours are contributing to less productivity and performance within the workplace. This also applies when working from home and the inability to shut down after work. Many employees check their work emails well past working hours, sending and receiving emails in total disregard for their colleagues' personal time. This behaviour results in colleagues receiving emails after working hours, affecting their wellbeing within the home or waking to a mountain of emails. This increases stress levels first thing in the morning. Employees or managers who send emails after working hours, especially late at the night, are the worst. I know, I used to be one!

Emails after working hours in the new normal must be heavily restricted to emergencies only, the same for working through breaks and lunch. The factors I noticed as a CEO for the 3 p.m. slump in the workplace were the lack of taking breaks, a person's diet (what employees eat/overeat at lunch), and a lack of physical activity and fitness. Three areas that require immediate attention and education from employers to increase wellbeing, avoid burnout and health issues with hybrid working. Employers must be mindful that employees working through lunch or outside of contracted hours could create complications from such behaviour that will have serious legal implications. The best practice for hybrid working is to have software attached to work emails that become active after working hours. The software can then track employee engagement outside working hours, and prompt or stop that employee. Employers can go as far as installing software that doesn't allow work emails to function outside working hours.

Management of employees within the home environment is a major topic for employers and managers, especially here in the west, where mental health issues in the workplace have increased for decades. A topic mainstream media, governments, and organisations have overlooked. The great resignation proves employers don't have that same luxury in the new normal. Organisations that overlook mental health in hybrid working will undoubtedly pay the price. The great resignation is a message to organisations that the status quo of modern work is unacceptable.

Economist Lawrence Katz describes the great resignation as "a once-in-a-generation, take this job and shove it moment," giving workers a once-in-a-generation upper hand. There's been many studies by think tanks and consultation groups on the causes of the great resignation. Their findings, although insightful, were obvious. I haven't found one study that's been a "eureka moment" in my research on this topic. Most conclusions on the great resignation point to issues that can be spotted with some common sense applied by a fit-for-purpose management team. Organisations must be mindful that the workplace issues created by the pandemic also affected management teams, and also require the human touch. Too much pressure will lead to oversights and human errors in managing people within the management team itself.

Anyone who pays rent, or even a mortgage, understands why the labour shortage and the great resignation are underway. If you take an overpriced city like London, where there are no rent regulations or controls in place, tenants who rent privately typically spend almost 40% of their income on rent. It gets worse for people on lower incomes, according to SpareRoom's research.

They report that a quarter of Londoners spend over half of their monthly income on rent, with one-bedroom apartment renters paying more than half of their salary on accommodation in twenty-five out of thirty-three London boroughs on average. Boroughs, such as Chelsea & Kensington and Hackney, came in at 85% and 81% of wages, respectively. People are working to have a roof over their heads, having to fund the rest of their lives with the pennies they have left.

This is a tragedy for young workers and the working class, especially considering decades of inflation, stagnant wages, energy prices, and the cost-of-living crisis. The Office for National Statistics in the UK (ONS) reported a 46% rise in the number of 20 to 34-year-olds going back to live with parents since 1999. They're known as the "Boomerang Generation" and "Generation Rent." Georgie Laming from Generation Rent in the UK said, "Young people are facing an impossible choice: either stay if you're lucky living in your childhood bedroom in the hope you can save a deposit – or rent and face a struggle to put money aside." Two-thirds of private renters have no savings. When you combine this situation with poor pay and defunct people management practices in the workplace, some reasons for the great resignation become clear.

If a business owner or a CEO was asked what they think would happen to an organisation where stagnant wages, poor pay, poor conditions, and poor people management practices were the norm, they'd confidently and clearly break down the consequences and serious implications for that organisation, showing off their business prowess. Yet, in the real world, some business owners and CEOs seem to overlook that fact within their organisations.

There's no place for this management lethargy and delusion in the new normal. The great resignation is living proof of that. If organisations want to get mental health and people management right in the workplace, they need to have face-to-face human conversations with their staff. It's impossible to get mental health at work and people management practices right, without that human connection and effort. Managing people over Zoom or Teams isn't a human connection and has its limitations.

In the new normal, CEOs and senior managers must stop hiding behind their work and job titles and get behind those they manage. Managing people in the new normal is profoundly based on common sense. If an organisation requires a think tank or third party to come point out the obvious, it's likely the management team in question lacks the common sense required for their purpose. Common sense, combined with people skills, is a must-have, to hold a role in management at any level and are relative to wellbeing at work. Employers shouldn't mistakenly think that common sense is a given, absolutely not, especially with managing people. As an experienced CEO, I can safely say that common sense is far from a given. If you're a senior manager who ignores what the middle and line managers inform you regarding the wellbeing and management of staff, you have a "can you just sort it out" mantra with your managers. You're one of the drivers of poor wellbeing at work that fuels the great resignation. Organisations and managers will require a plan of action on what needs to be done to reverse the great resignation. This plan of action must be unique to an organisation and the incumbent workforce. Don't look for an off-the-shelf generic solution for wellbeing at work. There's no such thing. With managing people, every organisation's challenges are unique as our fingerprints.

Even with MHFA training, many organisations mistake it for a tick-box exercise. Once the course is completed, mental health at work is sorted. Box ticked. The truth is far from that and there's a lot of work to be done after the training. Holistic people management, especially those focused on mental health and wellbeing, is a constant work in progress. A continuous journey unique to each organisation. Until organisations recognise this and get it right, employees are saying, in millions, that employers can stick their "bullshit job," their "bullshit people management practices," and "bullshit pay and conditions." The great resignation is a good indicator that employers have run out of time for scratching their heads, thinking about what to do, or putting off what needs to be done. The time has come to stop procrastinating and take action.

In April 2021, four million Americans quit their jobs, leaving 9.3 million job vacancies open according to the U.S. Bureau of Labor Statistics. Oddly, this happened when people were keen to get back to work after job losses, redundancies, lockdowns, and everything else we went through during the pandemic. August 2021 topped that when another 4.3 million Americans quit their jobs. In the UK, Brexit and the mishandling of its transition, global supply chain issues, and the impact of COVID-19 have led to major staffing issues. A survey of 6,000 workers in 2021 by Randstad UK, the world's largest recruitment company, found that around a quarter of workers planned to leave their jobs over the coming months. This was because of the high number of vacancies available and burnout due to the pandemic.

Around 69% were confident in finding a new role, and 24% planned to change employers within 3–6 months. It was a change from the usual 11% who would change jobs in any year. Randstad UK also estimated the cost implications of this for employers in the UK, to be around £25K for each worker. They advised employers to look at pay and conditions to keep their staff. That advice isn't rocket science, but it highlights the disconnect between employer and employee and the mutual needs and wants in that relationship. Any employer that needs a third party to come along and point out something so basic should be embarrassed.

I've mentioned the UK and U.S. a lot in this book, but the great resignation isn't a phenomenon of the West. This ideology is also taking shape in China. A movement coined Tang Ping, or "Lying Flat," has come into force. The young people in China, discontent and unhappy about the exhausting culture of working long hours for small rewards, and the need for a lifestyle change, started the movement. A lot of workers in China, like in the U.S., cannot afford their homes, even though they feel they are "living to work." China already has a shrinking labour market and an ageing population. According to CNBC, a world leader in business news and real-time financial market coverage, China will lose 70 million people from its workforce in the next few years.

By 2050, 330 million Chinese will be over the age of 65, making China one of the world's fastest ageing populations in modern history. There won't be any let-up for the young in China who will be expected to pick up the slack, causing a major crisis in their work-life balance. Young Chinese are unhappy with the way things are, they see no let-up for the future. The ideology behind "Tang Ping" is contentment in life, not being overworked, and having time to relax. Just basic human needs. Young Chinese are fed up with gruelling working hours and the constant consumption culture and are "lying flat" in protest by doing the minimum. Of course, the Chinese authorities have decided the movement is a threat to national rejuvenation and has censored it. Time will tell where that approach will take China.

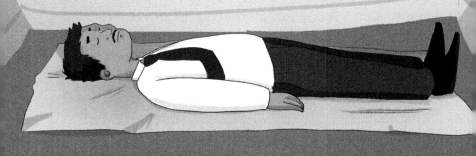

Tang Ping or "Lying Flat" Movement.

An interesting fact about the great resignation is that mid-career employees have the highest resignation rates. I've mentioned the mindset of younger millennials and the incoming workforce of Gen Z's and why organisations must adapt. The resignation rates in mid-career employees prove that discontentment in modern work affects all generations. This has major implications for employers. Mid-career employees fall into the age group of 25 to 45 year olds. This age group will make up most of the managers and experienced talent in any organisation. Losing these skilled workers is a disaster for employers. Employers are well versed on the detriment of losing key staff, such as experienced managers. The knock-on effect can go on for months, affecting wellbeing, productivity, and performance. The recruitment process to fill such a role can also take months, making each day a struggle until the right person is found. The departure of an experienced or loved manager leaves a gaping hole in skill and people management requirements. This can lead to discontentment in an incumbent workforce, which can slowly turn into a vicious circle of unhappy, underperforming staff, adding to the list of challenges for the organisation.

In the new normal, organisations need to start the dialogue to stop the rot or be overwhelmed with staffing and management issues. This is already happening in the UK in 2022, with flight disruptions in UK airports with staff shortages, train and postal strikes because of poor pay and conditions, and holdups at the border to the EU. As a CEO, my most productive times were when my staff turnover was non-existent, and the workforce was happy. I had five perfect years of zero staff turnover. My staff was happy with the pay and conditions, the culture, and the way they were managed. They also felt heard and felt their managers had their backs in line with their appraisals. The result of that was we saw 210% growth, leading to a turnover of £1 million for the first time in a financial year. The Made in Britain section of Business Matter magazine featured me regarding this growth in 2014. That was the tip of the iceberg of the positives. As a CEO, I have experienced first-hand the power of a happy organisation, a culture I insisted on and developed as a CEO. For me, simple common sense determined that, if my employees are happy, it would positively affect my bottom line. Employee happiness forms a major part of the psychological contract and is something I stumbled upon as a CEO, rather than something I knowingly worked towards. A place mutually beneficial, protective, supportive, and nurturing between the employer and the employee.

In the new normal, organisations need to be even more aware of the value of the psychological contract, as the relationship between employer and employee has deteriorated to an all-time low. I discovered a good example of this on Russell Brand's YouTube channel regarding Walgreens, an American company that operates the second-largest pharmacy store chain in the U.S. Russell Brand's YouTube channel is one of the most important and interesting sources of information on the internet. Presented in typical Brand fashion, funny, witty and engaging, on topics many of us are unaware of or disengage with, as we may feel powerless to influence them. The topics discussed won't only leave your jaw on the floor, it spells out the impact they have on everyday people.

Now, if you are British, Russell Brand can easily be sidelined or ignored. Everyone has an opinion about him, especially the mainstream media. I used to see Russell Brand in Shoreditch regularly from my office window walking his dog. I'd think, *Oh look, that t*at from Big Brother's Big Mouth, but the dog is lovely.* As with many people in the UK, I never regarded Brand as a person I needed to pay any attention to. And, in those days, I was probably right. He wasn't my cup of tea; a perception people have of Brand to this day. Brand, however, has come a long way since then and you're missing out if you are not engaging with his channel. Elon

Musk tweeted in March 2022 "With so many media companies saying @rustyrockets is crazy/dangerous, I watched some of his videos. Ironically, he seemed more balanced & insightful than those condemning him!"

I agree with Musk on his evaluation of Brand's channel and content. If you're not already watching, you should be, and we should hail Brand as a national hero for the content on the channel. The content on his channel isn't being discussed or debated in mainstream media, or in the format and style Brand delivers. It renders traditional news sources pointless since Brands content encourages a person to think, whereas mainstream news only seems to purvey what they want a person to think. It's a must-watch channel for everyone and one of the last few bastions of honest debate and thought provocation left in modern times, with a following of over 6 million subscribers.

Regarding the Walgreens case in the U.S., a California federal judge ordered Walgreens to pay back $4.5 million in settlement for employee wage theft. Walgreens rounded down employees' in and out times, shortened their pay, and refused to pay for skipped breaks and time spent during security checks. Now, for any organisation to sink that low, one would think there must have been serious debts or cash flow issues in order to consider stealing from employees, not that it would excuse wage theft. According to the Guardian, the CEO in charge for most of the time during the wage theft not only saw his compensation package rise from around $7 million in 2015 to $17.5 million in 2020, he was also promoted from CEO to Executive Chairman in 2021. A big pat on the back and promotion for corporate criminality, wage theft, and employee job misery. Walgreens also profited $2.5 billion in the 2021 fiscal year. At no point was Walgreens struggling during the time of the wage theft, so it begs the question. Why?

This isn't unique to Walgreens. Wage theft is a common problem in the U.S. A study done in 2017 in the ten most populous states found minimum wage violations, which is only one type of wage theft, affecting 2.4 million workers, accumulating $8 billion in losses to wages, around $3300 per worker. If we looked at these organisations' behaviour as people, they'd be described as thieves, robbers, people with distinct personality disorders, and self-serving narcissist psychopaths. However, they are organisations, so we look past that fact and don't refer to them as such. It does, however, question the mental state of the individuals that make these decisions, and the hierarchy that supports them. These decisions are taken, and a hierarchy lacking empathy and perhaps dealing with a host of personality disorders, greenlights them. An entire management team filled with self-serving narcissist psychopaths. It's a scary thought. If you look at it through the lens of mental health, it shows damaged individuals in desperate need of help, support, and therapy as humans. Not to mention some love, forgiveness, or perhaps a hug. When organisations have the audacity to function and think in that way, is it any surprise we have this great resignation?

On the flip side, I've found newer organisations that are impressive in their business operations and people management practices. I've accidentally discovered two organisations in the luxury watch sector in the USA.

The Timepiece Gentleman, a luxury watch dealer based in Dallas in the U.S. owned by Anthony Farrer and Marco Nicolini, is setting a benchmark for organisations to follow when it comes to the psychological contract. The Timepiece Gentleman is a classic story of how the marketing power of social media can create awareness and success for a brand. That's nothing new and, admittedly, Farrer's commitment to the brand and the lifestyle, and Nicolini's genius in classic watch history, are major contributing factors to their success. However, that isn't just where their true power and business acumen lie. It's in the psychological contract they've developed with their staff, which is at the heart of their success. Having watched their YouTube channel for over a year, the founders have implemented a masterclass in the application of Maslow's hierarchy of needs with their employees. It's great to watch the channel for their HR practices even if you're not into watches. It's clear that their reward and recognition process is the perfect balance of the transactional and the non-transactional.

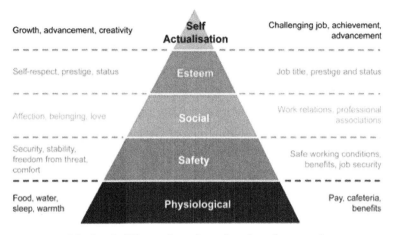

Maslow's Hierarchy of needs related to work

The interesting thing about this organisation is that neither of the founders has CEO experience, nor vast experience in people management or HR. They simply realise that, as people, we all have the same needs and wants and utilised that fact. By doing so, they've created a tribe/family of intrapreneurs within their organisation. The employees stand behind the owners and their vision, whilst creating their own plan of action and vision on how they want to contribute to the organisation as intrapreneurs. Farrer and Nicolini give their employees the autonomy to showcase their preferences and tastes in the products according to their personality via their social media feeds. This is a genius tactic. I already have my favourite member of their team, Victor Berry, who posts watches on his wrist on his feed. As a person of colour (POC), I can then relate to how it will look on my skin tone. I noticed Berry's demeanour and personality engaged me. That's made me like watches I never would've considered and that's great sales and marketing. What the Timepiece Gentleman has done is created a masterpiece in people management, engagement, motivation, and the psychological contract.

Employees can contribute purposefully and aren't micromanaged to the point the lose their identity. This is vital to the psyche and wellbeing of employees. The content showcases just how involved and empowered their employees are, and how the friend/family management style can bear fruit. It's through the Timepiece Gentleman I came across another luxury watch dealer putting out similar content. Roman Sharf and the content on his Grey Market channel also display a solid understanding and implementation of Maslow's reward and recognition process. The people management practices of these two organisations at the human level are great examples of what organisations, CEOs, and managers need to aim for in the new normal. The management style of these CEOs may not be everyone's cup of tea, or suitable for certain sectors, but there's plenty that employers and managers can learn regarding people management and the psychological contract. It's well worth a watch. Pardon my pun!

When an organisation gets the psychological contract right, the sky is the limit. I've found organisations in the new normal raising wages for staff retention as a reaction to the great resignation, incorrectly believing this is the only solution. A decent and dignified wage is the foundation for developing a great psychological contract in the same way MHFA training is the foundation of wellbeing at work. Employers unable to get that basic first step right, have no chance of creating or experiencing the benefits of a good psychological contract within their organisation.

According to Maslow's hierarchy of needs, humans are motivated by five essential needs: physiological, safety, social, self-esteem, and self-actualisation. With work, physiological needs include a good salary, good benefits, and a safe and comfortable working environment, alongside basic creature comforts, such as a staff room or cafeteria. According to the theory, if these first and most basic needs aren't met, employees will decide based on compensation, safety, or stability concerns. Therefore, organisations must ensure these needs are fulfilled before others further up Maslow's pyramid. Employers must remember that even though wages play a major role in job satisfaction and the creation of psychological contracts, pay is far from the be-all and end-all. There's more to consider.

There's a chain of thought that says, if an employer keeps raising wages, workers will just keep spending and remain in the same financial predicament. There may be some truth to this, hence why personalised financial management training and coaching should come as standard in employment contracts in the new normal. As the saying goes, "If you give a man a fish, you feed him for a day. If you teach a man to fish, you feed him for a lifetime."

According to organisational scholar Denise Rousseau, a psychological contract is more than the formal, written expectations between an organisation and the employee. A psychological contract comprises unwritten and intangible agreements between an employer and employee and evolves constantly based on communication. The psychological contract will include informal commitments, expectations, and understandings that underpin the formal contract. The psychological contract forms the backbone and the ongoing development of an organisation's culture. It's based on how people work together, mutual understanding, and respect.

There's no greater force within an organisation than the culture created by a good psychological contract, it determines staff retention, staff turnover, and attraction of new skilled talent. Developing good psychological contracts takes many checks and balances. Pay, wellbeing, work conditions, and managing expectations to get the formula right all play their part. As a CEO, I found using appraisals to identify the needs and wants of the employee, asking about personal issues, and not just using appraisals for target setting or transactional purposes was a winner. I set no time limit for the appraisal, provided unlimited coffee and food, and I was always on hand as the CEO if any member of staff wanted to speak with me during their appraisal. It was all organised prior to the appraisal. I saw appraisals as a chance to get to know my staff better. Inadvertently, it resulted in bettering myself as a CEO.

I received feedback from staff regarding myself as a CEO and how they perceived me. That was invaluable information and, as the years rolled on, my staff became more and more comfortable with the process. They seemed to relish the opportunity twice a year where they could tell me about myself in a safe space. I found it not only funny, but informative, and I loved the process. The feedback kept me grounded. I became more self-aware as a CEO and self-awareness is a major factor needed to be a great CEO. One of the most memorable lessons I learned about myself was when a member of staff pointed out that whenever they spoke to me, I always finished their sentences. They told me that when I did; it answered their question or helped them to get to the point quicker. It, however, left them feeling frustrated for not getting to the point quicker, leaving them feeling like a "child who cannot articulate," as one member of staff described it.

This came as a surprise. While I was aware I did this, I was convinced, when I did, it was a help rather than a hindrance. I could see where this member of staff was coming from. I learned that most of my staff were creative or artistic, also known as "right-brained" thinkers. They were hair and makeup artists and I learned I had to change my communication style with them compared to my office team. The office team were mostly "left-brained," analytical and methodical thinkers like me. I realised I had to be a different CEO with each group and each personality in my company. The only way I could do that was to get to know them better and use different facets of my personality to connect with staff on a human level. The more I got to know my employees on this human level and acquainted myself with their window into the world, the more natural the process became. It reminded me of Bruce Lee's quote "be like water." Being able to relate to individual employee realities, can be the determining factor in being a good CEO, or a great CEO. This applies to all levels of management.

We can relate individual employee realities to Jacqui and Aaron Schiff's frame of reference model. We all have a unique filter on reality, that is our window into the world. Our window is influenced by experiences in life, beliefs, and external factors unique to us.

Frame of Reference Model by Jacqui and Aaron Schiff

We all use our "window on the world" to define ourselves and others. As humans, we perceive the world, ourselves, and other people differently. This influences our behaviour and the way we speak and act, depending on where we are and who we're with. This is why most of us have an office/phone voice and use language and tone that differs when speaking with friends, family, and work colleagues. It's the same with our behaviours, which differ in a professional environment compared to a social environment. The footage of Finland's Prime Minister, Sanna Marin, having a great time with friends was a perfect example of this. Good on her, and it was great to see a politician being a genuine human!

There are many benefits to understanding the frame of reference and how it works for the better management of people. With many of my staff, especially my management team, I used this model to get to know their window on the world, as much as possible. That helped me understand their social characteristics and habits, rather than just their professional characteristics and habits. It resulted in a more personal and human connection with many of my staff. I found it broke down traditional professional boundaries, helping me to get to know them as people, rather than just employees. It helped me as a manager to appreciate why they think the way they do; do the things they do; and react the way they do with work-related activities. It allowed me to change the way I interacted with staff as I got to know what makes each individual tick.

During my transition to this way of individualised management, my left-brain thinking struggled with staff that took ten minutes to make a point or explain something that I could've said in a few short words. I'm sure this rings bells for some senior managers and CEOs. I'm sure you know my pain, especially when you're constantly busy, have an entire company or department to run, and nobody understands what that truly entails. I told myself it was work and to make a go of it. Slowly, the pain subsided into patience and, as I got more used to it, the process became easier to deal with. It also slowed me down a notch, which was a good thing. Ultimately, it not only made me a better listener, but a better CEO and manager.

I found this type of management style can lead to "TMI," or "too much information," and oversharing, especially on the personal side. From substance use to breaking the law, tax evasion, and relationship issues. Managers must handle this crossing of professional boundaries with care, as it can leave them in a predicament. As a manager, you must set boundaries where you don't involve yourself in any situation, that can be used against you. Common sense will determine where you'll need to slam on the brakes. Hence the essential skill of common sense in management. A great manager in the new normal must find a place with a well-balanced mix of both the professional, and the personal, with the people they manage. Set boundaries and stick to them. We all have needy friends, sensible friends, demanding friends, serious friends, and fun friends. A great manager in the new normal will play the sensible friend role.

As a CEO or manager, understanding the people that work for you, and getting feedback on yourself, is essential in the new normal. Be mindful that you don't reside in that place many CEOs and senior managers reside, where you've become too arrogant for feedback. A place where you feel there isn't much an employee can teach you, where you're comfortable with who and where you are professionally. I'd like to remind those CEOs and managers that the comfort zone, is where dreams go to die. Letting staff know you're available goes far in creating a top-notch psychological contract.

When my employees requested me to be present at appraisals, I took more of a listener role than the boss/CEO approach. Appraisals were more of a social event than an interview-like process. We did two appraisals each year with every member of staff. Time-consuming, yes, but also profit and productivity increasing, is what I found. We redeveloped appraisals so employees could see what we needed on our side as an employer. We then identified employees' needs so they could feel happy and supported, to deliver what was required of them. A true two-way street based on Maslow's hierarchy of needs. It helped that Maslow's work infatuated me during my MBA. If you work in HR or a management role and haven't come across Maslow's work, it's something you should educate yourself on in the new normal.

The information gathered over several years from the appraisals is the number one reason we had great psychological contracts and trust. The people management framework subsequently developed with the data from appraisals was the main reason my little SME beat the global competition for the Investors in People Award. I remember going to the award show with my HR manager. We sat at a table of ten with a company and the CEO of a huge multinational corporation who was also up for the same award. The CEO had flown in his management team from Switzerland for the show. I sat there wondering how a boy from Plaistow ended up as a finalist and was going up against such big organisations for such a prestigious award. I remember sitting there thinking, *is it this simple?* I also remember noticing there were only about ten people of colour in a room with about three hundred people, and wondering where were all my people at?

The finalists were ENGIE, a French multinational utility company with a revenue of over €60 billion; Oyster Partnership, a market-leading recruitment agency specialising in property across the public and private sectors; Salix Finance, a provider of government funding to the public sector. Companies all with managers with extensive management experience compared to myself; and, finally, London Hair and Beauty Limited, my little SME. Ultimately, the best HR framework and people management strategy that won, was the one my team and I created, under my guidance and vision as a CEO. That award-winning framework wasn't rocket science. It was common sense based on the understanding of how we function as humans. That award-winning strategy was built by doing one simple process. Actively listening to employees, then doing what needed to be done with the information gathered.

Active listening is a hard skill to master, and I'm still mastering it. It's a journey rather than a destination. As a reader of this book, a quick test you can do to see if you are a good listener is to ask yourself these three questions:

1. Are you a person who finishes other people's sentences?

2. Are you a person who plans a response in your head while a person is speaking to you?

3. Do you jump in mid-sentence when someone is speaking?

If the answer is "yes" to any of these three questions, you are a bad listener and by default, this doesn't make you a good manager. If you answered "yes," you can confidently give yourself an "F" for failure with your active listening. A "yes" to these questions proves that you listen to respond, not to understand. This a huge flaw as a manager and in general in society these days. This lack of active listening skills makes connecting with others a struggle. As a CEO, or if you're in any level of management, a lack of active listening skills plays a major part in the disconnect with those you manage. A personality trait you may be oblivious to, or you recognise but choose to ignore.

Disconnection is one of the main drivers of the great resignation and more than likely why, at the time of writing this book, Goldman Sachs headquarters in New York only got 50% of their workforce back to the office on a 5-day basis since the lockdown lifting. The CEO described remote work as an "aberration" that needs correcting quickly. Where I stand on the matter is that such CEOs are the only aberration that needs correcting in the new normal. Active listening is a skill covered in depth in MHFA training. It's one of the steps in the MHFA action plan. The purpose of the action plan is to listen actively, in order to spot signs of poor mental health. Applying that skill goes far and wide in general life. Therefore, I push any CEO and manager to take MHFA training.

People at the topflight of management can become so accustomed to people listening to them, they lose the ability to listen to others. When a person achieves a certain level of success, they can develop a mind frame where they think they know more than they do. Socrates said, "I know that I know nothing." That is the mind frame all CEOs should take in the new normal. A CEO open to listening in the new normal will embark on a journey of unlearning and relearning. Those who don't are in a dangerous place as professionals. Ego and arrogance are key drivers that prevent a person from evolving. The world of work is fluid and constantly changing, like the mental health continuum. What you may have known, and what worked last year, can become non-functioning the year after, evermore so this side of the pandemic. If you've been doing the same thing, or held the same role for many years, you're in more danger than most of falling into this trap of ego and arrogance. In the new normal, where everything has changed, the working world requires fresh new thoughts and direction in leadership. As a CEO or manager, this is the perfect moment to tell yourself you know nothing and start unlearning, learning, and relearning to be an effective leader. No businessperson or manager is above that process.

There are no experts in the new normal. To be an expert, you need years of experience in your field. The new normal is too new, is still changing, and will continue to change for the foreseeable future. This will be the case until pandemics are no longer a threat and we have final details of what the new normal looks like. Therefore, CEO or not, you're not an expert in the new normal. We're all a bunch of people trying to figure things out. When you look at things from this perspective, it's easier to humble yourself. You'll quickly realise that we're all at the same level in hierarchy and knowledge with managing people in the new normal, regardless of the job title. If you are a CEO, a manager or someone who has held your job role for many years. Do you feel you have nothing to learn about mental health and wellbeing? Do you believe it's all just some mumbo jumbo? If so, you're part of the problem. This is mental health and wellbeing. It applies to every job role that exists.

Your wellbeing affects everything you do in your life. MHFA is a course every CEO and manager on the planet must take. It helps to gain more of a real-world perspective on people and to support the changes their management teams identify, for better people management. As a CEO or manager, you're responsible for your next in line, all the way down to the office junior. Many CEOs and senior managers have forgotten that fact. MHFA training brings everyone in an organisation down to a human level. I love when a CEO joins a group of learners in my courses. For me, it means the training isn't a tick-box exercise, but a tool for real change. It helps the entire organisation connect on a level that is the common denominator for us all. Being human!

I watched an interview with Steven Bartlett on YouTube, by Link Up TV. This is a must-watch interview and Steven makes insightful points about CEOs which are relevant in the new normal and applicable to all business leaders and managers. Steven said, "CEOs should go to therapy, because the biggest predictor of failure for a CEO or founder is something that happened to them on the playground when they were a kid, which made them insecure. Due to this, they make decisions through that lens of insecurity." I believe this to be the case, not just on the school playground, but in the playground of life. He went on to say, "These insecurities can result in treating others like shit, they don't have the humility to receive feedback and the capacity to acknowledge their weaknesses." I found this comment insightful. It makes you wonder what happened to some of the billionaire business owners as kids to be the way they are today. Billionaires who are rich enough to reverse the current job misery in the working world with a click of their fingers. Start changes to save the planet with a click of their fingers, yet choose not to. Steven said that CEOs and founders should go to therapy if they want to be better CEOs and founders, as their egos and insecurities are hindering their success.

Listening to Steven say this struck a chord with me. Had I been in therapy and understood the mental health continuum when I was a CEO, not only would I have been better, but I may never have developed mixed depression and anxiety disorder. It made me realise that, despite my achievements and success, I never reached my true potential as a person or as a CEO. I hadn't been to therapy ever, yet led quite a traumatic life before I became a businessperson. I'll never know how that affected me as a CEO or as a person, but I'll make damn sure such oversight of my personal growth will never happen again. Steven also talked about Ben Francis, one of the founders of Gymshark, an apparel company worth over 1 billion. Ben Francis stepped down as CEO when it had thirty employees and spent six years working with every single team at Gymshark while the organisation was going through phenomenal growth in that same period. He then stepped back into his role as CEO, once he felt he had the knowledge to be the best CEO he could be for the company he founded. That's a perfect example of the humility, mind frame, and approach required in CEOs, managers, and business leaders for future prosperity in the new normal.

Steven Bartlett is now on Dragon's Den in the UK, and the Den's youngest ever investor at 29 years old. I used to love the Dragon's Den when it first began and watched it religiously. However, over the years, it lost its appeal. As a successful owner of an SME myself, knowing how hard it is to get a business to a place of success, I wasn't happy watching small business owners looking for investments and having to give away more than they wanted for their business and innovations, for a negligible financial investment from the multi-millionaire Dragons. For me, it became more about multi-millionaire businesspeople saying, "give me, give me, give me, more, more, more. And if you don't like it, it makes no difference as I'm already rich," and "you need me," type of feel. Over the years, it seemed geared towards making people who were already rich, richer from the hard work and innovation of small business owners by throwing pennies at them, it didn't seem fair. Everything we need to move away from in the new normal.

When I heard that Steven Bartlett would be on the Dragon's Den, I was pleased. Steven didn't disappoint with his first investment with a cheese maker who came in for a £150K investment and was offering a 3% stake in the business. Peter Jones, the richest Dragon on the panel, made an offer but wanted 15% of the business. Steven Bartlett also made an offer saying, "I'm not going to suck the blood out of you like Peter did," and made the same offer but for 7.5% of the business saying, "because I think that's fair." I almost spat my tea out all over my cat at that comment. Now, please don't take this as a put down of Peter. He was doing what the generation he comes from always did. I am a big fan of Peter Jones, and he's always been my favourite Dragon. Steven has a long way to go before he takes that spot. Peter also said to Steven that his percentage will get higher as time goes on, and it has. It was great witnessing the banter between old school and new school.

We need fresh new thought in the business world. Finally, I witnessed the future of business on my TV, the change in thought I'd been waiting my whole life to see. I hope this thinking Steven Bartlett displayed is contagious and inspires a new generation of businesspeople to come up with better ethics, morals, and care for the human element throughout the business world. I also hope it does the same for the generation of CEOs, business owners, and managers that come from that older cloth. I don't doubt it will, as I don't think there is a choice. In the new normal, it's not about how much wealth a person has accumulated. Net worth is a statement of repulsion. The word "billionaire" is repugnant due to the gulf between rich and poor, and it represents pure greed for the working class. In the new normal, "net worth" doesn't impress the everyday person. What impresses the everyday person is how those individuals dealt with others while they accumulated that net worth. I believe the human element will play a major role in seeking the right investors in the future and I wish Steven and his new company all the best.

Employers and CEOs must lead and drive the changes required in the new normal, shareholders can also play a major role. I've spoken with dozens of managers over the last three years, desperate to bring more people-focused management practices to their workplaces. I'm coming across this more and more, which is great news for employees. The pandemic has helped mental health and wellbeing finally get on the priority list in workplaces. That trend is gathering serious momentum here in the UK. I've noticed how bookings for MHFA courses skyrocketed between 2021–2022. This is a sign of things to come and great news for employees. The issue I've come across is that forward-thinking managers that want to bring in change after the training courses, are shut down by senior management and CEOs who have not taken the training.

It reminds me of the climate issue, where all the signs of climate change, the damage it's doing and what needs to be done to counter it, have never been clearer. Yet, at COP26, the menu was 60% animal-based. According to the UN, meat and dairy cause, 14.5% of global greenhouse gas emissions and 45.1 million hectares of land have been deforested between 2001-2015 by the beef industry. Yet a bunch of dinosaurs approved the menu for what was essentially the most urgent climate conference in the history of humankind. You would've assumed that someone in the management at COP26 would've made the connection. The result of COP26 was that governments and big corporations made big promises as they always have done at every COP, and decided they'll carry on as they have been for the foreseeable future, before bringing in the urgent and necessary changes needed to save our planet. The COP is almost three decades old and look where we're with the planet. It's probably why Alok Sharma was really crying at the end of COP26, and Greta Thunberg describes the COP as a scam for the biggest polluters in the world to greenwash the climate crisis. The point I'm trying to make is that with organisational change in the new normal, talk, promises, and half-hearted initiatives will blight organisations the same way it's evidently blighted the outcomes for COP for almost 3 decades. Let's hope they can at least get the menu right at COP27, I wouldn't hold your breath!

For many organisations, the year-end profit, targets, and numbers seem to supersede everything else, with hardly a thought spared to the potential consequences of quick profits and results. Quick profits and results do not allow for the long game, where leaders and managers can look at other aspects of a business to identify areas that require attention that can impact performance and profits positively. It seems when an organisation makes a profit, they conclude they've found the pot of gold at the end of the rainbow. They only need to work everyone harder to make even more profit. In the new normal, shareholders, CEOs, and decision-makers must redefine what profit is. They must realise that profit and sustainability aren't only found on their balance sheet, but abundantly in the happiness and wellbeing of their employees. Employee wellbeing has a major impact on the bottom line and it needs to be mined for growth. For this to happen, organisations must focus on the human element. Managers must feel they have the full support of their seniors to bring in the bold changes needed in the new normal. I've spoken with many managers who feel they're asking for a huge favour when asking their employer or senior manager to fund anything to do with wellbeing in the workplace. In the new normal, leaders should actively encourage practices within their management teams to improve wellbeing at work, and be happy to pay for it. We already know it's not a cost, but an investment with a five-fold return, and endless benefits for the employer and the employee.

In the new normal, shareholders must have more of a say in the business model of organisations and people management practices they're invested in. Shareholders should push the wellbeing at work agenda as a priority to their CEOs. In doing so, shareholders will force the changes needed in the new normal to happen more rapidly. It will help plug the trend of the great resignation and general job dissatisfaction, making the organisation more attractive to employees and profitable. Organisations must accept that their responsibility to employees and shareholders are the same. Organisations won't find a better potential for growth and sustainability in the new normal than in the area of employee wellbeing. Staff wellbeing is the real pot of gold for any organisation and one that's been overlooked for generations.

Visier, a software solutions company for workforce analytics and workforce planning based in Vancouver, Canada, found that the top six reasons people quit their jobs in the great resignation were:

- Reason #1: They've got a taste of work hour flexibility
- Reason #2: They're burned out
- Reason #3: They're not feeling connected to the company culture
- Reason #4: They want to continue working remotely
- Reason #5: They don't see a clear path forward
- Reason #6: They want to spend their time focused on doing meaningful work

This list isn't exhaustive and, depending on the organisation and sector, the reasons will differ. This list highlights the changing nature of employees in the new normal and the need for dialogue and the establishment of a "happy place" between employer and employee. It highlights a new era of people management that requires employers to recognise and act on wellbeing. Whether you're a manager or the managed, ask yourself how the organisation you work for is addressing the issues raised by the great resignation. The answer will let you know whether you have the right leadership in place for the new normal, and how much work needs to be done regarding people management within your organisation.

The great resignation is globally protesting "job misery" it cannot be ignored. There's been a spiritual awakening over the pandemic, and millions have decided that a job isn't the most important thing in life, especially if it makes them unhappy. Indoctrination of the ideology through school, college, and university that work, and careers, are the highlights of a person's life is changing rapidly. Employers need to be aware of this change and adjust. Many have, for many years, felt trapped and exploited by their work and they're in open rebellion. On Reddit, there's an anti-work forum of over a million people discussing workplace issues and pushing each other to quit their jobs, a sign of things to come, perhaps. Organisations should take this ideology seriously and not mistake it for a passing trend. If your organisation isn't discussing the issues I've mentioned in this chapter, and how it can adapt to cater for this shift in the mind frames of the modern workforce, your organisation is being run by the wrong people. Those dinosaurs again!

5

The Race Issue

Race and wellbeing for people of colour (POC) go hand in hand. Being informed and literate on the race issue is one of the most powerful tools an organisation can have in their management arsenal. If an organisation is based in a city like London or New York, where around 40% of the city is non-white, or anywhere there's an incumbent diverse workforce. Being racially literate is an obligation for any CEO and manager. Any manager who thinks managing a Black person, a White person or another POC requires the same skill set couldn't be more mislead. As a manager, remember that White people don't all fall into the same category, either. Eastern Europeans face high levels of racism and discrimination in the UK that impacts their wellbeing at work, and many don't even speak English in some sectors, such as construction. There was a spike in hate crimes against Eastern Europeans following the Brexit vote in 2016. A study by the University of Strathclyde revealed that 77% of Eastern European pupils suffered racism, xenophobia, or bullying, and 49% said attacks increased after the Brexit vote. Therefore, even within the White workforce, there are diversity issues employers and managers must be aware of that impact work life.

With POC, the first thing organisations can do is stop using terms like BAME (Black Asian Minority Ethnic) and referring to people of colour as "ethnic minorities." This type of terminology adds to the general disenfranchisement of these communities. The fact is, Black people and POC may be a minority in the UK or the U.S., but with around an estimated 8 billion people on the planet, 7 billion are POC. Globally, these communities are the vast majority and extremely diverse, they represent a huge majority of the global workforce. With race equity training and diversity consultancy in the West, where a diverse workforce is an aim or a fact of life in recruitment due to the local demographic. It's essential to ensure that racial diversity consultancy comes from, and is led by, POC or a team who are truly diverse.

A no-brainer you may think, but there are organisations being consulted on Race at Work by organisations or teams that are White-led and have a White majority. This can be due to the data they use which is gathered directly from POC communities or think tanks. Therefore, White consultants and organisations feel they have enough facts about race and diversity to be consultants. My advice to organisations and managers that consider this ridiculous path, is to get out of the mind frame, that doesn't allow you to see a POC as an expert. That is racism. An organisation can stop this nonsense by finding a high-end POC who works in the field to consult and train your organisation. There's plenty out there!

The acceptable terminology for organisations to use in 2022 is "Black people" and "people of colour," or "Black communities" and "people of colour communities." Be warned there are some POC who don't like the term "people of colour," usually because of generational racial experiences and history. The word "colour or coloured" was used during segregation in the USA and apartheid South Africa. Many people of colour are still alive from that era, generations that came after are not familiar with that experience. Organisations can also use a term I first heard from Ama Afrifa-Tchie who is the head of people, wellbeing, and equity at MHFA

England. On a webinar, she used the term "People of the Global Majority" which I fell in love with the moment I heard it. People/Person of the Global Majority (PGM) should become the default description for POC in the new normal. I encourage organisations and individuals to use it.

Compare that term to "ethnic minorities" or "BAME", you can see how PGM is powerful, positive, and uplifting, while the other two are side-lining and minimizing. Be warned, this terminology may change, and organisations will need to change with it. A consensus within your organisation on terminology, to discover what language everyone is comfortable with for race identity, is best practice. Once again, don't forget to involve all the PGMs within your organisation in that consensus. Ultimately, what they say, goes. Organisations may find the language deemed acceptable will be unique and specific to them, due to factors such as age and perceptions of words and terminology. Using unique and specific language accepted internally is best practice when it comes to being racially literate as an organisation. It will give all employees the confidence to speak on racial issues with accepted and correct terminology.

The reason Black people, Black communities, or people of African descent or diaspora must be viewed and managed uniquely compared to other PGMs, is because their experience of racism and discrimination has been far more intense in modern history. White supremacy has always been rooted in, and upheld in anti-Blackness, therefore it's essential to distinguish Black people and their experience from other PGM groups. Organisations and managers need to clearly appreciate this fact. Racism and discrimination play havoc with mental health in PGM communities, negatively affecting all aspects of life including work. Coming from the PGM community myself, having lived experience of what PGMs in the UK have faced when it comes to racism, discrimination, and mental health, I can confidently say that racism, discrimination, and mental health are inextricably linked. My whole life, wherever I go, even up to today, I must always keep in mind the colour of my skin. That's just a fact of life. It supersedes everything else in all aspects of my life. This is due to my lived experience of racism and discrimination.

The consequence is that I'm constantly aware of what White people might do, say, or think about me because of the colour of my skin. This is the case no matter where I go. Everyone has their idea of what White privilege is. For me, White privilege is never having to keep the colour of your skin in mind, not in the West anyway and not anywhere it matters. As humans, we all struggle in life, life is hard enough and takes its toll on everyone. As a PGM, we must deal with racism and discrimination as a non-optional extra on top of everything else. I feel that's what's most unfair about racism and discrimination. Employers must be aware that all PGMs experience racism and discrimination and it can lead to mental health implications.

Mental Health First Aid England (MHFAE) persistently pushes the anti-racist agenda at work in the UK. Lead by the unapologetic Simon Blake MBE, who has a long history of allyship championing causes of the young, PGM and LGBTQIA+ communities. His vision as CEO made MHFAE one of the leading lights of the anti-racist movement, one which relentlessly pushes for a seismic change with diversity and inclusion in the UK. MHFAE found that an enormous amount of work is required to dismantle systemic racism and remove the racial gaps that impact mental health. Their progress report on race equity and anti-racism revealed that the understanding of race, racism, anti-racism, and race equity are key drivers of the cultural, workplace and systemic change needed in mental health in society for PGMs.

Their findings for Black people and PGMs showed racial inequity impacts every aspect of life. Exactly as it's been for me since childhood. Reading the report was enlightening. I've always felt my experience with racism was a demon unique to me. The report showed that my experience was a common factor for most PGMs which helped normalise my experience to a degree, making it easier to come to terms with. MHFAE found, in the workplace, 50% of Black people have faced racism, and 29% said their mental health was affected at work because of that experience. Also, 70% of PGMs have claimed they've faced racial harassment at work in the past five years and 33% of Black employees feel their race is a barrier to promotion or their next career compared to 1% of White employees.

Here in the UK, there's a huge problem with racism, institutional racism, and discrimination in the workplace. A problem with a substantial negative impact on an organisation's bottom line and the economy. It is not only creating mental health issues in PGM employees, but it is also costing businesses dearly. Route2, an organisation that empowers employers for systemic and sustainable change, alarmingly found ethnic discrimination in the workplace costs the UK £40 billion annually. That equals 1.8% of GDP and £10 billion more than Rishi Sunak's coronavirus response package. Racism is expensive! The new normal presents us with a massive opportunity to get things right and leverage the opportunity found in racial diversity. It will undoubtedly take new thinking in leadership and management, and it's clear from the data available that current leadership within many organisations in the UK and the USA, are failing miserably.

My first experience of racism happened at eight years old in primary school. Being a child of first-generation Sri Lankan immigrants and coming to live in the UK as a six-year-old in 1984. I used the name "Rishi" at school, which is what my family called me. Whenever someone asked for my name, or it was called out, other kids would laugh. They also made fun of my accent and for not speaking English well. At that age, I didn't realise I had an accent or if I was speaking correctly. I'd come from Sri Lanka in the mid-80s to London, and into what seemed like a world of racism that I didn't understand or comprehend. At such a young age, nothing seemed right, and it was all confusing. Kids in the playground made fun of my name and I eventually wished I had a "normal" name like everyone else. Half the time I didn't know why they giggled and laughed at me, so I'd giggle and laugh too.

Even the Black kids who laughed at me had "normal names." At that age, Black kids having similar names to White kids confused me. In the mid-80s most Black kids were from the Caribbean. These were children of the Windrush generation. They were more British than other immigrants as they'd been around longer. Even though they were Black, they spoke and acted like White kids. Of course, I wasn't aware of the Atlantic Slave Trade and how Caribbean people inherited their European names at the time. All I knew was I wanted one. Ironically, they also used to laugh at my surname, Perera, which is European of Portuguese origins and stems from the colonisation of Sri Lanka.

As an adult, I know this was my first experience being marginalised and bullied because of my background, leading me to feel low, confused, and inadequate. I didn't realise "bud bud ding ding" was a racist slur for almost a year, even though I heard the phrase almost every day as a child. In fact, it was a Pakistani boy named Isan Akram, who explained everything to me, he was notorious in primary school for always fighting and being a "badboy". He took me under his wing and let me know clearly, I would also need to be a "badboy" to survive.

It makes me wonder how damaging it was to go through that at such a tender age. Little did I know that racism would become a major part of my life experience and have a profound impact on whom I became as I got older. Funnily enough, "Rishi" is now the name of the British Prime Minister. Rishi has become a name you read or hear on TV every day. How times change!

My name over the years was "whitened," without me even realising it. As I explained, my family calls me "Rishi" and over the years my friends, both White and non-White, slowly changed that to Richie. It started happening in my early- to mid-teens and was a slow, natural, and unnoticeable process. I spared no second thought about how my name changed to Richie. Since my teens, through my entire career, and to this present day, Richie is the name I use without giving it a single thought. Writing about this metamorphosis of my name and the mental metamorphosis of my mind, I've realised using this more "whitened" version of my name has made my life over the years that much easier. I guess I eventually got the "normal" name I always wanted as a kid!

Now, what's interesting about name "whitening" is that, in a U.S. resume study, economists Marianne Bertrand and Sendhil Mullainathan found that White-sounding names, for example, "Emily Walsh," received 50% more call-backs for interviews compared to Black-sounding names, for example, "Lakisha Washington." Even though candidates were equally qualified. The study estimated, painfully, that being White gave employees the benefit of a person with eight years more experience than equally qualified Black candidates. A breathtaking head start!

The Harvard Business Review published Sonia Kang's work in 2016, that reported, PGMs are aware of prejudice due to their names. PGMs thus counteracted this by masking their names or information on their CVs, which may give away their ethnicity.

Some 31% of Black professionals and 40% of Asian professionals admitted to "whitening" their names for better interview prospects. Sonia Kang then conducted a follow-up experiment to see if "whitening" resumes work. Kang sent 1,600 applications that were "whitened" and "non-whitened" and ensured that half of the companies were actively seeking diverse candidates. The study found that even with organisations apparently "actively" seeking diverse candidates, whitening résumés increased call-back rates from 10% to 26% for Black people and 12% to 21% for Asian people.

Unfortunately, with a quick bit of research on Google, these organisations are easily exposed. The incoming workforce of Gen Zs will do their homework on their employer, actively avoiding organisations that lie to keep up appearances. This information makes me wonder about all the extra benefits I may have received in my life by simply changing the "S" to a "C" in my name. It's incomprehensible that something this irrelevant could result in me either getting, or not getting a job, or playing a part in influencing my successes. Whether I'm Rishi or Richie, I'm the same person, the same professional, with the same skill set and achievements. This may seem ridiculous if you're White, but it's a reality for PGMs. As a reader of this book, if you wonder why I've crossed out "Richie" on the front cover and written in "Rishi"? Well, now you know!

I attended Vicarage Infant and Junior School in East Ham. I was around eight years old when I heard the word p*ki from another kid, a little older than me at school, for the first time. I didn't even know what it meant. I remember looking at the kid, wondering why he said that. I was learning English, so perhaps it was a word I hadn't learned. Ironically, it was a word I'd become very familiar with growing up in Newham in the mid-80s. From primary school onwards, my experience with racism became more intense, but eventually, I reached a milestone. I knew what it was, that it existed, that it was dangerous, and what warning signs and behaviours to look out for. This is probably why I'm someone that notices everything. It can be a gift and a curse, but when applied correctly, it gives a huge advantage over the next person. It's also an excellent and powerful skill to possess as a manager.

From the age of ten onwards, my experience with racism became more extreme when we moved from East Ham to Plaistow in East London. In those days, racism was an everyday part of life, so much so that "NF" (The National Front) used to be graffitied on walls everywhere. On buses, on desks at school, and even in the toilets at the youth club as a constant reminder of who you are, and where you stand. Racism in those days was violent, brutal, and in your face. You had to prepare to run the gauntlet for it every day. Being prepared was the deciding factor between being racially abused verbally or coming home black and blue from a full-on beating.

I grew up on Prince Regent Lane, with the nearest junction with Barking Road being the Greengate. The junction was named after one of the pubs on the corner, opposite another pub called the Castle. Both pubs were notorious and two of the main drinking spots for National Front members, West Ham United supporters and the notorious ICF.

The ICF, also known as the Intercity Firm, was the most feared football hooligan faction in the UK in the 80s and early 90s; and supporters of West Ham United. People who were hard as nails and well-versed in dishing out a thorough beating. The NF and the ICF were the groups I feared the most as they walked around in packs.

Growing up around racists in East Ham and Plaistow was confusing. I learned racists would ignore you or give you a nod as you walked past them on the street when they were alone. Yet they'd beat the life out of you on another day, or if they were in a group. There were a couple of occasions when racists from my area got into arguments because one racist was unhappy with his mate racially abusing me. It was because I was friends with his little brother, or they knew my mum was a nurse at the local hospital, or that I was local. Some would stop to talk to me, stroke my dog, and offer me cigarettes. They'd ask what team I support, and I would say, West Ham, they would respond "good boy." This was my life from the age of six to about thirteen. I got into many fights because of someone being racist toward me. I realised I could fight, and I was good at it. I was always getting in trouble, especially at secondary school for fighting. Eventually, my fear subsided and my reputation as a person to be left alone in my area grew.

In fact, it was an extremely racist NF older boy from East Ham, who first showed me how to fight. I have no idea why he liked me, or even took the time to talk to me. He used to tell me if anyone was racist to me, I should punch them in their face, or he'd beat me up. I took this seriously as I feared him. As I got older, people got to know me in Plaistow, and things got easier. People I knew were racist, or had racially abused, or had beat me up in the past, would say "alright mate" and tell other racists to leave me alone, saying "he's alright" as they walked past me on the street.

This was why growing up, racism and racists were confusing for me and why I've never hated or disliked White people for my experience. How could I, when fifty per cent of the racism I experienced or witnessed throughout my life was perpetrated by PGMs? This internal racism I experienced was never as violent or hateful, but it was still racism and just as damaging.

My experience of racism made me realise that even racists have a good side to them. They're like everyone else, products of their environment and victims of what they think they know. Therefore, I believe racism is associated with a lack of education that leads to ignorance, mental health issues, substance abuse, personality disorders, and social issues. These experiences however made me tough, fearless, and strong, traits that have contributed to my successes and achievements in life. Sometimes I feel almost grateful for it, as I got to know a side of me that is strong, fearless, and resilient. It could also just be deep-set trauma I'm yet to deal with.

Before things got easier for me, growing up, all racist factions were the same. Whether they were NF, West Ham, or ICF, I avoided them at all costs. It wasn't worth the risk of trying to figure out who was who. That was, however, easier said than done as the A13 motorway split my road, Prince Regent Lane, in half with Custom House on one side, a no-go area for me. I remember having to take the bus through that side of Prince Regent Lane to visit my sister in North Woolwich. There was always a gang of around thirty skinheads outside the Londis mini market that seemed to be there 24/7. The bus stop was also outside the Londis, which made the situation more precarious as it gave them easy access to the bus. Every time the bus stopped there, my heart pounded, hoping they wouldn't get on the bus. Thankfully they never did. As a kid, it was terrifying, as any eye contact, even for a fleeting moment, could cause a severe beating as it had frequently growing up. With our house being on the main road, it was one of the main through routes along with Barking Road that skinheads from Custom House and Canning Town would use to get to the pubs and West Ham United's ground at the time, The Boleyn.

As a child, on weekends and match days, gangs of skinheads marched past our front door chanting "Ding Dong the lights are flashing, we are going p*ki bashing." We had a brick thrown through our window into the front room once, which was nothing compared to what our Indian neighbours experienced a few houses down. I'm sure people from that era can remember the rest of that song, the lyrics I'd rather spare the readers of this book. The thought of what would happen if I was outside would terrify me. As a South Asian, I was their prime target. During that period of my life, leaving my front door was an obstacle course in avoiding racists, a skill that all kids of colour had to develop without a choice on the matter. In this book, I won't get too deep into the amount of racial abuse I experienced as a young person, as I could write a book on it. However, being spat at, called p*ki, and having coins and eggs thrown at me for walking down the street was everyday life.

All the kids of colour took beatings by racists, but Asians from the Indian sub-continent were the main targets. It was only verbal abuse if you were lucky, or perhaps a slap or a punch. If you were unlucky, you'd be hospitalised or worse. Racists killing Stephen Lawrence in Eltham, Southeast London in 1993 only became national news due to the police trying to cover it up. Racist killings have happened in the UK many times, up and down the country. From what I remember, the police were just as racist in those days and, from what I hear from young PGM, especially Black boys, today, nothing much has changed.

On one stop and search, a police officer told me not to touch the door handles in his car, as he didn't want a brown stain on it after sitting me in the police car to check my license. I may have been eighteen years old at the time. I just laughed it off, as being racially abused was expected, and I was totally desensitised. I also knew he'd be lying flat on his back if it wasn't for the uniform, and that made me feel better. I guess racial abuse instilled violence in me from a young age as a coping mechanism. It was one of the many occasions the police racially abused me. I was once threatened with arrest because of being born in "la la land" according to one officer, after reading Sri Lanka as my birthplace on my driving licence.

Ironically, my father was a Metropolitan Police (MET) officer with over twenty years of service and retired from the MET. He was a PGM officer when casual racism was part and parcel of British culture. Due to the dinosaurs in the Metropolitan Police and the Independent Office for Police Conduct (IOPC), along with brutal cuts to frontline services that have seen London become one of the most dangerous cities in Europe, nothing much has changed. If anything, it's getting worse. Recent events at Charing Cross Police station found evidence against officers for rape jokes, homophobic, misogynist, racist comments, and disability discrimination that came to light. More recently, they stripped and searched a fifteen-year-old Black child (Child Q) while she was on her period without informing her parents. Child Q was stripped searched at school by MET officers and forced to remove her sanitary towel.

The Metropolitan Police and their issue with racism have been well documented with report after report, and have been ongoing for generations. The government has now put the force under special measures for falling short of getting the basics right, damaging the confidence of Londoners. The Metropolitan Police are the perfect example of the outcome for organisations when dinosaurs aren't removed, and fresh forward-thinking leaders aren't appointed. If this goes on today, I can only imagine what my father's lived experience of racism was like, working for the MET all those years ago.

Writing about my experience with racism, I came to realise we never spoke about racism as a family. I'm unsure of my mother's experience with racism, or my siblings. In hindsight, I can see we left everyone to deal with racism alone as a family growing up. Perhaps it was too embarrassing or traumatic to discuss. I wonder if it's a common theme not to discuss racial abuse in PGM families in those days, like avoiding discussing mental health nowadays. Recently I discovered Idris Elba moved from Hackney to Canning Town when he was fourteen-years-old. Canning Town, in those days, was more than likely the most racist area in London, and a dangerous one. An absolute no-go zone if you didn't grow up there. I could only imagine what Idris, as an outsider Black boy, had to face. His experience in the area would've been the same as mine. I'm sure he could second the extreme and brutal racism that PGM had to endure in those days daily. Looking back now, it was so extreme it doesn't seem real, even after living through it. PTSD? Maybe.

The consequence of this experience is that I keep in mind the colour of my skin wherever I go. It's so deeply embedded in my psyche. When I walk into a roomful of new people in a new environment, my "racistdar" is the first thing that turns on. I'll instinctively look for body language, facial expressions, warning signs, signals, or off-the-cuff remarks of potential racism. My "racistdar" isn't something I purposely turn on; it happens naturally, like a natural defence or survival mechanism. It's always there, like my vision or my hearing. It uses up my energy and lowers my frequency when that energy could be used for something more positive. There's no way for any human to experience racism and discrimination and not be affected by it, leading to character traits, flaws and wellbeing issues.

Today, racism may not be as normalised or blatant in everyday life. However, it's had a revival because of Trump and racist comments made by former Prime Minister Boris Johnson. When it's "OK'd" at a high level, it gives racists a platform and a green light to come out of the woodwork, profoundly affecting PGMs. I am sure many PGMs were surprised at comments being made by some of their White friends and colleagues on social media during Trump's presidency and George Floyd's murder. I certainly was. These days, racism is more undercover, delivered via microaggressions and the safe spaces it finds in social and work environments. According to Forbes, microaggressions come in three forms: microassaults, microinsults, and microinvalidations.

Microassaults are when a person knowingly speaks or behaves in a racist manner and uses racist symbols. An example can be someone who knowingly makes a racist joke and are fully aware that it is racist, yet claims it's harmless. Microinsults come in the form of verbal and nonverbal actions that demean a person's racial background via rudeness and insensitivity. A person that uses microinsults can either be aware or unaware of their racism. An example of this can be when a White employee expresses astonishment at how a PGM got their job, implying they didn't get the job on their personal merits. Microinvalidations are actions or behaviours that negate, exclude, or ignore a person based on their race. People guilty of microinvalidations usually deny that they were being racist. An example is asking a Black person where they are from, a question they would not ask a White Person, implying they don't belong.

It makes me wonder if today's racism is more insidious. At least the racism I experienced was clear as day. I could see it coming from a mile away. The insidious nature of microaggressions in the workplace is that white co-workers may gaslight PGM's and deny any wrongdoing claiming they are being sensitive or have a chip on their shoulder. For PGMs, racism evolves and raises its ugly head generation after generation. Each time it does, there are mental and social consequences.

I feel it's important for me to tell my story about racism and how it's affected me personally. I've spoken to White people and even have White friends who struggle to realise the impact of racism. Some even deny that systemic and institutional racism exists. Almost like it's something PGMs woke up one morning and invented. "You know how they like to moan," "they've all got a chip on their shoulder," "why don't they just try harder," and "nothing is ever enough." On many an occasion, I've heard White people discuss the race issue using this type of terminology. This is racial gaslighting and is the driver of an important factor currently ignored in diversity and race equity training. This factor is called White resentment. White resentment is associated with White people being opposed to, or resentful of, any racial or diversity practices and policies.

White resentment causes disengagement and disenfranchisement on policies and progress, both in the workplace and in society, on anti-racism. For any White person reading this book who struggles to understand how racism affects PGMs, I hope my personal experience has shed some light. You have only to place yourself or your child in my shoes at any stage of my life from six to fourteen years old. Then ask yourself, if you or your child could've walked away unscathed. Racism is like a man knowing what labour pains might feel like, because a mother explained it. A man, however, would need to be a woman and a mother to truly understand. It's the same for a White person to understand what racism really feels like.

White resentment is the reason many White people deny there is White privilege, systemic racism, or racism and discrimination in its most basic form. Michael Norton and Sam Sommers' study in 2011 found that 57% of all White people in the U.S., and 66% of the White working class, see racism against Whites to be at the same level as racism against Black people and PGMs. I'm sure some PGMs will be shocked, frustrated, and even angry at these findings, coming from a country built on the genocide of Native Indians and the enslavement of Africans. It's easy for PGMs to brush such data off as nonsense, but to make progress with the race issue, it's imperative to acknowledge that everyone has their own filters on reality.

White resentment is why the All Lives Matter (ALM) movement came into existence. Of course, All Lives Matter, that's the whole point and the reason the Black Lives Matter (BLM) movement came into existence. A connection that hasn't been made by the ALM camp. BLM exists because of the random and frequent killing of innocent and unarmed Black citizens by the police in the USA. A deadly situation that required global attention and one that didn't affect White people in the same brutal fashion. Due to White resentment, many White people got the idea that BLM meant White lives don't matter. If all lives truly matter, this same camp should protest about the lives of those being bombed in the Middle East, the Uighurs in China, and the apartheid in Palestine. What about the lives of those living in the "Jungle" in Calais, Mexican children getting ripped away from their parents and slung into cages, the lives of refugees drowning in the English Channel? When someone shouts, "all lives matter," who exactly is "all lives"? With BLM, it's clear and specific. If "All Lives" really matter, one cannot be selective in what "All Lives" represents. If all lives matter, that should, by default, include Black lives.

This brings it back to individual filters on reality, and once we make that connection, it makes the debate less about being right or wrong, or Black or White. It makes the debate about a lack of understanding of viewpoints and issues, on both sides of an argument, which requires a safe space for dialogue. Some PGMs won't entertain the fact that the obvious regarding racism and discrimination, must be spoon-fed to some White people.

This can and does make PGMs frustrated and angry, which is understandable. The fact is, the obvious sometimes still needs to be pointed out. As a PGM if you're not willing to do that, then you must recognise you're a part of the problem, no matter how frustrated you may feel.

The viewpoints that fuel White resentment are real to those who hold them, as much as race issues are real to PGMs. These viewpoints will continue to cause issues within organisations trying to implement anti-racist practices. A robust anti-racist campaign in the workplace won't only focus on the issues PGMs face, but also on understanding the causes of White resentment in order to dismantle that ideology via awareness and education. Any approach to anti-racism is flawed if White resentment and White issues with anti-racism policies aren't acknowledged.

White People can also experience racism from PGMs, this racism may not be as hateful or misguided as White racism towards PGMs, and never led to historical crimes such as slavery, colonialism, genocide and imperialism against White People. For some White people however it still exists, and it can fuel White resentment towards anti-racism and diversity policies. With race equity training, White resentment must be addressed in an intersectional fashion to reform the understanding of racism and its impact. If this doesn't happen, White resentment will ensure that the dismantling of racism in all forms remains a losing battle. For PGMs, it's the same as banging your head on a concrete wall, hoping the wall will break. The only result is a concussion. PGMs have banged their heads on this concrete wall for generations regarding the race issue, for what can be seen as slow to little progress. It's time to try something new!

To make a real breakthrough regarding anti-racism and diversity issues in the workplace and society, PGMs must change their approach and think outside of the box. When the race issue is discussed or taught, PGMs must be mindful that it doesn't feel like the race issue is being rammed down the throats of White people. Remember to keep in mind, it is a subject some White people simply can't comprehend. If they cannot comprehend it, that doesn't make them by default racist, it just makes them human. PGMs need to be mindful that if the race issue is always put forward in a way where the perception is PGMs are victims, and White people are perpetrators. It will continue to cause disengagement and resentment.

For some White people, PGM issues are as hard to comprehend as it is for PGMs to comprehend the findings of Michael Norton and Sam Sommers' study. This conflict of realities has been going on far too long and is regressive and polarising. As PGMs, we have an obligation to educate White people on the race issue, but it must be done so they can engage, too. Intersectionality is the correct approach to the race issue, where equal rights for PGMs don't come across as fewer rights for White people, or an opportunity to tell White people how awful they are.

I'm connected to two cities, Liverpool and London. In both cities, many White people live below the poverty line most of the month, and feed their families in food banks. Try explaining to them and their families how they benefit from White privilege and how they're in a better place in the world because they're White. They'll look at you and wonder what on earth you're talking about. Some White people feel the same way about race and diversity issues and policies. Some just don't understand it, and it seems some PGMs just don't understand that. This disconnect is why the race issue has gone around in circles, generation after generation.

In the new normal, it's time to try a different approach to diversity. To do that, organisations must provide a safe space to discuss all forms of racism. This must include racism that White people have against PGMs and understanding White resentment and how to dismantle it via education and dialogue. It must also include the racism PGMs hold against White people and the internal racism that PGMs have towards each other. This then levels out the playing field and the race issue then becomes an all-inclusive subject instead of a Black Vs. White issue. When this happens, White people will engage the race issue in a much healthier manner. Racism is racism, no matter who the perpetrator may be. We must address all racism with the same level of priority. If this approach isn't taken, PGMs risk being labelled as hypocrites in their quest for an anti-racist world. None of us can change the past, but we sure can change the future.

I am sure there are White people reading this book whose employer has been on a "diversity drive," or has committed to diversity and may feel a bit sidelined. White people who don't have a racist bone in their body, but still feel that everything seems geared towards supporting PGMs. White People who feel they're being ignored and marginalised and fear speaking out in case they're labelled a racist. Speaking out or asking questions doesn't make someone a racist. It's simply someone's reality that requires addressing if we're to find true progress on the race issue. To see the changes that PGMs have been fighting now for generations to come to fruition in the West, White people's allyship is essential, White people must be on board.

With the race issue, throughout history, there's been White allies ready to die for the cause. Let's not forget White people went to war with each other, fought, and died in the American Civil War to abolish slavery. It was White people who knocked down the statue of slave trader Edward Colston in Bristol. There are White people just as angry at colonisation, slavery, oppression, systemic racism, and discrimination as PGMs are today. These are true allies, and they're much needed. Like it or not, countries like the USA and the UK are White countries. PGM are a tiny minority, with little power or influence where it matters.

When PGMs do get into a position of power, we get the likes of former Home Secretary Priti Patel, happy to send PGM refugees to Rwanda and welcome White Ukrainian refugees with open arms. The most racist law that's been passed in my lifetime. Therefore, it's extremely important for PGMs to build channels that are engaging and educational to their White counterparts. Without that White engagement, PGMs will continue going around in circles, trying to make the race issue something that's taken seriously by the majority, rather than the minority.

Without majority White allyship, the changes needed won't see the light of day in the West. If this all-inclusive approach to the race issue isn't taken, organisations will solve one issue while inadvertently creating another. I'm sure that some White people reading this are relieved that I've raised these points. They may have certain concerns or misunderstandings about the delivery or need for anti-racist practices in the workplace, but may not speak on it, in case it sounds, or comes across as racist. However, it's a conversation that must be had within organisations. Establishing healthy anti-racism practices in any form will need both Black and White cooperation and understanding. It will take some effort to find that happy place. But with collaboration and understanding, it's an absolute reality.

The race issue must be addressed in workplaces through training and continuous professional development (CPD) via unbiased and inclusive education on the subject. Organisations should seek to create safe places for these discussions with set rules of conduct. This is how a diverse organisation, or an organisation trying to become more diverse, can embed an anti-racist culture into their workforce and get all employees firing on all cylinders. Bianca Jones of EDP training in Bristol is a shining beacon in raising awareness on race issues in the workplace. EDP is an organisation based in Bristol delivering Race Equity courses directly linked to MHFA training. As I've mentioned before, the two are inextricably linked for PGMs. Race equity training is the building block for any robust anti-racist, educational, and inclusive framework that organisations must develop in the new normal.

As I've mentioned before, racism isn't just a White Vs. PGM issue. Racial issues within PGM communities must be tackled as fiercely as the approach taken to deal with White racism. It's not only White people that can be racist, and we must be crystal clear on that fact. All people can be racist. I've experienced racism from both White and Black people, including other Asians, in my life. I've witnessed this internalised racism within PGM communities first-hand. Growing up in London, especially East London, the social implications of diversity and poverty are things you become well versed in. Employers and managers must recognise that internalised racism exists and must also be addressed within the workplace. PGMs can be racist towards White people and other PGMs. This internalised racism sometimes feels like an unspoken issue in PGM communities. It's usually brushed aside or laughed off and dealt with nonchalantly compared to White racism. Racism is racism, and any form of it must be dealt with head-on. It can never be justified that PGMs wouldn't accept racism from White people, yet are nonchalant about racism within their communities. That's hypocritical. Racism should never get a pass in any form in any community.

My first experience of internalised racism was in my community as a Sri Lankan. Growing up, I witnessed a lot of racism between the Sri Lankan Sinhalese community, the Sri Lankan Tamil community, and the Sri Lankan Muslim community. To this day, this racism exists and intermarriage between these communities is frowned upon or deemed unacceptable by some. Inside Southeast Asian communities, racism is rife, and one consequence is "Honour Killings." According to the Honour Based Violence Awareness group, people committed honour killings as a tool for controlling behaviour. They're a way of protecting cultural honour and beliefs to stop shame towards a family or the community. Honour killings target both men and women, with women being more commonly targeted. Honour killing is based on cultural racism, they could murder an Indian person who may be Sikh for marrying a Hindu or a Muslim and vice versa. This is common in Asia and there have been many honour killings here in the UK going back generations.

There's a deeply ingrained racial tension between Indians and Pakistanis. I've witnessed racism between Caribbean and African people, to where I've heard Caribbean people say they "hate Africans." Even within the Caribbean community, I've heard Jamaicans referring to other Caribbean's as "small island," a derogatory term to imply that people from smaller islands in the Caribbean have smaller minds. I've heard comments from African people about how Somalian people are "not Black." Even within Muslim communities as local as London, I've come across many an Arab or Asian Muslim man or woman forbidden to marry a Black Muslim, especially if it was a Black Muslim man.

PGM communities can also look down on a PGM marrying a White person. In fact, this is quite common. Examples of internal racism within PGM communities are rife, and on occasion, as violent as White racism. If it's not OK for White people to be racist and PGMs are pushing for change, then should there not be the same push for change to end this internal racism? As with White resentment, race equity training must encompass an awareness of internal racism within PGM communities, for it to be fit for purpose in the new normal.

The Impact of Cultural Stigma on People of the Global Majority Communities

In some parts of Asia, the Middle East, and Africa, mentally ill people are still shackled, caged, imprisoned, and even tied to trees. Some are viewed as possessed by demons and left to roam the streets as a warning to others. Those archaic practices may seem like a world away. However, the mindset of that cultural stigma toward the mentally ill has a long and powerful reach. Black people and PGM represent a community with a broad range of cultural, racial, and religious differences that are deeply ingrained. These differences impact the perception of mental health in various ways in each separate community.

PGM communities represent around 13% of the UK, around 8 million people from about 66 million. Black people and PGMs are three times more likely to develop mental health issues, yet are the least likely to seek help compared to the general population. This approach to mental health naturally leads to mental health conditions going from mild, to moderate, to severe completely unnecessarily, and has a substantial impact within these communities. If you're from the PGM community, this should strike a chord with you. As a member of this community, it certainly does for me. This type of data represents the toxic cultural perception of mental health within PGM communities, which has been around for generations and is firmly embedded in the culture. Racism and discrimination exacerbate this toxic environment. Employers and managers need to be aware of this and keep a closer eye on the mental health and wellbeing of their PGMs.

If we consider the Chinese community in the UK with a population estimated at around half a million or 0.7% of the population, the Chinese Mental Health Association seems to be one of the very few organisations putting out any information regarding mental health in the Chinese community. When I was doing research on mental health in the Chinese community, I was surprised to see such a lack of information and transparency in mental health data for the Chinese. There were two or three organisations catering to half a million Chinese in the UK. That's concerning as the community has faced an explosion of discrimination due to COVID-19.

The Chinese Mental Health Association was the most informative website I could find on Chinese mental health statistics in the UK. Since the pandemic, they've removed their website. If other organisations cater to the Chinese community in the UK, they're not readily available or visible online. I managed to dig up some data on the Chinese community in the UK. According to the Chinese National Healthy Living Centre, language, culture, poor symptom recognition, and stigma are often cited as barriers to access, leading to low uptake of mental health services.

The NHS Executive Mental Health Task Force report observed that the Chinese and Vietnamese communities were largely 'invisible' to mainstream purchasers and providers.

The main areas of difficulty for Chinese families were:

- Lack of English
- Lack of knowledge of their rights
- Cultural differences, including lack of understanding by the statutory sector
- Scattered settlement
- Long and unsociable working hours

They found that Chinese people were more likely to be classified as having a severe lack of perceived social support. Social support is significantly associated with wellbeing and recovery. Mainstream mental health services in the UK know little about the mental health of the Chinese community. Up-to-date information is almost non-existent. This isn't surprising, as the Chinese conceal mental illness for fear of losing face. They attribute mental illness to character flaws and hereditary issues. "Face" in Chinese culture is viewed in relation to the whole family rather than to an individual, thus the stigma, shame and loss of "face" extends to the entire family. Chinese philosophies have shaped Chinese concepts of health and mental health, as much as Chinese medicine. All these issues in the Chinese community are a perfect example of one community and its unique complexities. It's evidence we cannot group mental health support into a generic approach for PGM communities.

The Black Caribbean and African populations represent around 3.3% of the UK population, around 1.8 million people. Caribbean and African peoples' cultures are uniquely different, even though the two are always put together. In contrast to the Chinese community, there are specific and mainstream mental health services available to the Black community. Yet statistics are frightening!

According to the Mental Health Foundation:

Detention rates under the Mental Health Act are four times higher for people in the "Black" or "Black British" group than those in the "White" group. Does racism have a part to play in this statistic? The risk of psychosis in Black Caribbean groups is estimated to be nearly seven times higher than in the White population. Whilst the White Caucasian population experienced the highest rates of suicidal thoughts, suicide rates are higher among young men of Black African, Black Caribbean origin, and middle-aged Black African and Black Caribbean women. Heartbreakingly, they found that the influences on the Caribbean and African communities' mental health were:

- Racism and discrimination
- Social and economic inequalities
- Mental health stigma
- Criminal justice system

As you can see with Black and Chinese communities, even though it is the same topic of mental health, the situation on the ground is like comparing apples and pears. Therefore, it's important not to lump a group of people together due to background. With mental health and wellbeing in PGM communities, segregation is the best practice. For organisations and managers, it's best practice to be well-versed in individual and specific information on mental health for each PGM community. This extra effort in the new normal will ensure no one gets left behind in the world of work, leading to better leadership and management through awareness.

Black People and PGMs in the UK represent 13% of the UK population, so you might be surprised to know the community represents 21% of the NHS workforce. According to the UK government website, there's a higher percentage of staff in medical roles (working as doctors in hospitals and community health services) from Asian, Chinese, Mixed, and Other ethnic groups than in non-medical roles. The mainstream core of the NHS is heavily invested in PGMs and omnipresent at all levels. So, with all that intelligence, medical background, experience, and knowledge in the mainstream medical field, why are PGM communities in the UK the most likely, not to seek mainstream help with mental health?

It seems PGM in the UK are happy to work in and play a major part in the mainstream medical sector, yet with mental health, they shy away. Could it be that generational cultural stigma? Whatever it is, any employer with a racially diverse workforce, or employers seeking to make their workforce more diverse, must push the agenda on mental health with all employees and provide extra provisions for PGM employees. This isn't special treatment; the data shows it's required. This is a good example of the education, reasoning, and explanation needed, to dismantle White resentment towards anti-racism. This extra provision for PGMs is not favouritism, it's a prerequisite due to data.

Employers in the new normal should encourage employees to seek help and support for their mental health and create frameworks to normalise this process. Employees who are open and honest regarding their wellbeing, and are receiving the help and support they need, will always be more valuable than an employee that hides their mental health issues. For communities of colour, this internal push by employers to seek help and support for their wellbeing will also affect their communities outside of the workplace. Stigma, lack of understanding, shame, and fear of mental health issues in PGM communities create an overwhelming impediment in how PGMs deal with their mental health. Many PGMs don't have a safe space to talk within their homes and communities. This stigma runs so deep, I can even relate it to my own family who are all well-educated, UK-based, and westernised.

If you consider the level of education and professions within my immediate family circle, one will never guess a stigma would exist on any topic, especially one as important as mental health. My family has deep-set roots in healthcare, with my mother and all my aunties working and retiring with the NHS. I've written extensively about my mental health journey over the last few years. I've launched an organisation in the mental health space as a reaction to my illness and my life-changing recovery process. Mental health and wellbeing is something I promote on my social media pages. Yet not one member of my family, immediate or extended, has approached me to ask what happened with my mental health when I fell ill. Seems improbable, right?

The stigma around mental health runs so deep for many PGM families they cannot even approach the subject. It's that taboo. I'm sure a lot of PGM reading this right now would've experienced similar situations within their own families and community. I fear for future generations of my family if this approach to mental health doesn't change, and for all other PGM families who struggle with tackling this subject. What I've noticed since I launched Mental Health and Life was the number of friends and acquaintances on social media that have approached me regarding their mental health, all with the same issue of feeling isolated. Even one of my uncles who helped to raise me came forward and took on training.

Now, on the flip side with my family, if it was a physical health issue, it would be the extreme opposite. The response would be an overload of dialogue, information, and check-ins, exactly like when I got COVID. The phone didn't stop ringing to check up on me and give me advice on what needed to be done to get well. I even had aunties calling me from abroad to discover if I was OK and to give me some "get well" advice. The absolute opposite of when I was diagnosed with mixed depression and anxiety disorder. Not one conversation was had with any member of my family regarding this. Until they read this book, they'll never know that on several occasions, it took me to a place of suicidal ideation. What we need in PGM communities is not more GPs, lawyers, accountants and businesspeople, we are overloaded with those. We need more therapists, counsellors, neurologists, mental health professionals and all other types of head doctors. I pray the younger generation acts on this.

Ironically, the same strength and resilience I discovered through my experience of racism, that helped me to understand that I'm not made of glass. That I can handle a lot of stress and pressure and come out the other side fearless and strong. This resilience was one of the main contributing factors that got me through the recovery process with zero family support. I'm far from the first person in my family that's had to do that. That same strength was the reason I was brave enough to write this book and talk about my experience with mental ill health. I guess that's why they say, it's a funny old world.

A lot of PGM keep their mental ill health quiet, too embarrassed to even discuss their recovery. This stigma deletes narratives of hope and belief, and stories of recovery that are critically lacking and invaluable. This lack of narrative leads to a vacuum of essential information and insights not being available on mental health, mental ill health, and recovery that are significant for any community to be healthy. This is a tragic situation caused by stigma and toxic perceptions of mental health that is taking a huge toll on Black and PGM communities. "We" must do everything we can to dismantle this stigma, as this is a medical emergency. I use the term "we" as this shouldn't just be a PGM effort and issue. Everyone can play their part, White and Black, including managers and employers.

There's a lot PGM communities can take from the White Western world with mental health. The West is pushing the agenda on mental health like no other part of the world and creating a global awareness. The rest of the world seems stuck in the dark ages. There's no arguing about that fact. Therefore, I'm a big fan of cultural appropriation. In fact, as a species, it's how we built nations and civilisations. Cultural appropriation has a bad image, as it can be done callously. PGMs can perceive cultural appropriation as White taking from Black, but it's not all one-way traffic.

If you are a PGM living in the UK, what language are you reading this book in right now? Where were you educated? What accent do you have? What's the main language you speak? What currency do you exchange when you visit other countries? What passport do you hold? Do you support a football team? Where do you feel most at home? For me, the answers to these questions simply fall under England and British, as it does for many PGMs living in the UK. Is this not cultural appropriation?

I certainly will be culturally appropriating or even culturally appreciating my Western education on mental health to enhance self-care, kill stigma, and advocate the topic of mental health for everyone in the UK. I'll also be taking this education back to Sri Lanka to change perceptions and the status quo around mental health there. My goal is to set up MHFA Sri Lanka soon, so any toxic perceptions and stigma regarding mental health can be resolved at the root cause for Sri Lankans. This will ensure that future generations of Sri Lankans worldwide won't have to experience the cultural shame and stigma attached to mental health. This will make the global Sri Lankan population much healthier in the future. As children of immigrants, is this not the reason our parents ultimately came to the West? To better ourselves, appropriate what's good and beneficial and take it back to our country of origin for the betterment of our people? Is that not the true purpose of an immigrant? There are too many PGMs calling foreign countries their home, whilst their country of origin is in dire need of the value and skill set, they acquired in a foreign land.

With mental health, it's imperative that PGMs take this approach. The issues with mental health and PGMs aren't solely a UK issue. It goes back to wherever you're from as a PGM. So, appropriate what you can and change things for the betterment of your people. This is the best way to flip the script around mental health so that in the next decade, PGM communities globally will have a totally different perception of mental health.

This mind frame should apply to everything for PGMs. If you're unhappy with institutional racism, mental health stigma, the political system, or any other system that doesn't work for you in the UK, or your country of origin. Your only purpose should be to become a part of that system and change it to how you want it to function. Some may consider this insurmountable, but they've forgotten those that came before. Let's not forget about the life and times of the one that conquered all his enemies and told us. "It always seems impossible, until it's done," Madiba.

The stigma, cultural shame and associated consequences are experienced by billions of PGMs worldwide. My story I've shared should give you a clue to how deep the rabbit hole of stigma around mental health runs with PGMs, even in an educated, successful, and westernised PGM family such as mine. I feel that, besides myself, my family has nothing to teach the next generation regarding self-care and mental health. It's a generational curse many PGM families struggle with and need to break, as the consequences are clear in the data. One of the reasons I wrote this book, is that I wanted it to be a story of recovery that future generations of PGMs can refer to. Letting people know, that no matter where you are from, we can discuss mental health. For PGM communities, these narratives and stories of recovery must become commonplace within our homes and communities.

It was good news when I heard one of my nephews, Nadeem Perera, is trying to address some of these issues through his organisation, Flock Together, co-founded with Ollie Olanipekun. You may have come across Flock Together on the BBC's The One Show. Flock Together is a birdwatching collective for PGMs. They have six pillars which include building community, challenging perceptions, showing the benefits of nature, championing ecological protection, offering mental health support, and providing creative mentorship for the next generation. These spaces are essential for PGMs to address cultural stigma in mental health and create safe spaces for open dialogue. PGM communities need more young people to step up and create spaces like Flock Together. This will ensure PGMs create narratives for the future on topics such as mental health for younger PGMs. They've also written a book, *Outsiders, The Outside is Yours*. The book goes into Nadeem's and Ollie's experiences of racism and how it affected their well-being, along with their love of birding and the importance of getting in touch with nature as a PGM.

Rethink Mental Illness, a mental health charity in the UK, found that in PGM communities, the barriers to getting help were that mental health issues aren't recognised, or seen as important culturally. This shows a lack of understanding by PGM communities on the impact of mental ill health. PGMs feel there's a lack of experts from their ethnic backgrounds who can understand them. They feel White healthcare professionals will never understand their experiences of racism and discrimination throughout their lives. They would be correct in thinking that. PGMs also feel that White healthcare professionals consciously or subconsciously think PGMs with mental health issues are angry or aggressive. Rethink found that shame associated with the cultural stigma of mental health was also a barrier to seeking help.

For many PGMs reading this chapter, it will ring many bells. An employer who develops a robust framework for anti-racism and mental health support for their PGM employees won't just be contributing to their overall performance and success, but also changing the status quo of the damaging cultural stigma and perception within PGM communities regarding mental health. Great news for an employer's corporate social responsibility. They will attract the best talent from the PGM workforce to their organisation, which is more important than organisations currently realise!

The Case for Racial Diversity in The Workplace

Now, some employers and managers may read what I've presented in this chapter about the management of PGMs and think, "Whoa! With all these challenges and effort required, why bother? Why not just employ White people and avoid opening this "can of worms" Well, let me tell you why!

The case for racial diversity in the workplace is profound, with the World Economic Forum stating, "the business case for diversity in the workplace is now overwhelming." As Guider, a mentoring and career development platform reported, employers with diverse management teams see 19% more revenue. Diverse boards saw 43% increased profits, and diverse organisations are 70% more likely to capture new markets. People Management, one of the UK's leading HR Media brands, analysed 200 management teams across a range of sectors and found diverse teams make better business decisions 87% of the time and make faster and better decisions 60% of the time.

PricewaterhouseCoopers reported that 85% of CEOs with a diverse and inclusive workforce noticed increased profits. The Boston Consulting Group, a global consulting firm, found that diversity of leadership teams leads to better innovation and better financial performance. They discovered that people from different backgrounds viewed problems in different ways leading to better problem-solving. This diversity solved issues, increasing the chances of one solution being effective. This comes back to how we all have a unique window on the world and our unique filters on reality, and why these differences are a cause for celebration, not division.

As you can see, having a diverse workforce is a must for any organisation serious about success. The extra management requirements for PGM are negligible when considering the benefits and impact a well-managed diverse workforce can have on an organisation. Employers should consider whether they can afford to miss this boat in the new normal, even with these statistics readily available that present a solid case for racial diversity in the workplace. The penny still hasn't dropped for many organisations. Probably, those damn dinosaurs again!

According to the Economist, LinkedIn has around 6,500 employees, around 5% are Latino, and 3% are Black. Google's workforce is 26% Asian, 3% Latino, and 2% Black. Intel's workforce is 8% Latino and 3% Black. No Black women CEOs lead any Fortune 500 companies, with only Mary Winston who held a role for six months, and Ursula Burns, who was the first Fortune 500 Black CEO in 2009. This is eyebrow-raising as the list started way back in 1955. Only 3% of Fortune 500 companies share their full diversity data and 60% of Black executives in Fortune 500 companies claim they work twice as hard, and produce twice as much, to be seen on the same footing as White colleagues on their level.

On the flip side, according to the U.S. Department for Education. Asian Americans have the highest rates of graduation at 74%.

According to the U.S. Census, 43.8% of African immigrants achieved the most college degrees, followed by 42.5% of Asian-Americans. Black women are the most educated group in America, even though they represent only 12.7% of the U.S. female population. Black women are coming on leaps and bounds in the USA, representing over 50% of Black people with post-graduate degrees. They outpace White women, Latinas, Asian/Pacific Islanders, and Native Americans in this arena. Therefore, it's surprising that Druthers Search, an organisation that helps companies with diversity and inclusion recruitment in the workplace, reported PGMs are more likely to be overqualified compared to White ethnic groups, yet White employees were more likely to be promoted!

This situation isn't just an American thing. The UK has a problem with discrimination within organisations, too. Chinese, Indian, and Pakistani names are 28% less likely to be called for interviews. Yet, Chinese and Indians have the highest educational attainment in the UK. Chinese students achieve the best grades in English and Maths. Indian students perform the best in languages, and Chinese students score the most 3As in A-Levels. According to the UK Government website, more PGMs attend university compared to White British students, and Chinese and Indians consistently are at the highest end of grades achieved.

However, when we look at how organisations leverage this educational resource, only 2.6% of tech board members are PGMs. Only four people on the boards of the UK's top technology companies are PGM. The financial times reported in February 2020, that 37% of FTSE 100 companies had no non-white members. The UK-based Economics Observatory found little change in pay, employment, and unemployment for PGM groups in the UK over the last twenty-five years. In fact, for Black, Pakistani, and Bangladeshi men and women, pay gaps compared to white men and women have widened. An insightful study by Carnegie UK trust found, that Black, Asian, and minority ethnic young adults are at a greater risk of being unemployed than White young adults. PGM groups are more likely to be in precarious work. They also found significant links between employment status and mental health in PGM groups.

I'm not pushing the systemic racism agenda here, just presenting facts. Understandably, organisations will have more White employees as this data comes from White majority countries. Yet, the small minority of PGMs incumbent within organisations in the UK and the USA, doesn't represent the ability, capability, and size of the demographic available as a workforce. It also questions if the size of the demographic matters when you consider quality over quantity. PGMs are at the highest level of quality with employability both in the UK and USA, if education is a factor. Having racial diversity in the workplace is like choosing between fast food, and a healthy balanced meal, and knowing the implications of both. Organisations are still choosing the fast-food option.

There are other factors to consider, such as the mindset of the incoming workforce of Gen Zs, who actively seek employers with wellbeing, inclusion, and ethics as core values. Organisations must work hard in the new normal to cater to the needs and wants of this generation or lose out on the best future talent. In fact, Gen Zs represent the largest generation, surpassing millennials globally. In the U.S., 47% of Gen Zs identify as Black Indigenous and People of Colour (BIPOC). According to Tallo, a USA-based industry-leading diverse talent network, 69% of Gen Zs responded "absolutely" when asked if they're more likely to apply to organisations geared towards racially and ethnically diverse practices.

When it comes to racial diversity, the data points towards discrimination in employment and promotion, prompting a few pressing questions for current business leaders and management teams.

- Is this racism or a lack of knowledge of the benefits of a diverse workforce?
- How damaging is a non-diverse strategy to the success of an organisation?
- Does a personal preference for the background of an employee, supersede the needs of the organisation?

As we come to the end of this chapter, I'd like to give the English Premier League a huge shout-out for still taking the knee before every game in solidarity against all forms of racism, social injustice, and discrimination in society. The BLM movement is no longer "the in thing," and long ceased trending and being cool on social media. The significance of premiership football players still taking a knee before every game, shows that true allyship isn't about jumping on the latest bandwagon, it's about staying consistent in the support of a cause. Well played lads!

6

The Vaccine Issue

The vaccine issue divides people and opinions and is a topic that cannot be ignored in the workplace or everyday life. Like the race issue, we must create a safe place for dialogue on this topic. Vaccinations add to the long list of ever-growing issues we face as a species that anger and polarise us. It seems that, as a species, we've developed a harmful habit of always finding new ways to be divided and angry. Is it a form of self-harm or are we continuously pitted against each other via the news and social media on this topic?

With the topic of vaccinations, the need to be right has once again superseded reasoning and conversation. At a time, we should all come together after experiencing the global trauma of the pandemic and lockdown, many world leaders (mostly all dinosaurs) have quickly reverted to their regressive thinking patterns regarding the vaccine issue, dragging us all down with them. In vaccines, we've found another war and enemy to fight that continues to divide us. So much so that there have been worldwide protests since governments and organisations have mandated vaccines. We may be on the brink of war with China, and Russia has invaded Ukraine. How ridiculous are the people in power in today's world, considering we're still gathering ourselves from the pandemic? Leaders in organisations can learn a lot from the mistakes made by leaders in the political spectrum, instead of following them off a cliff.

Now, whatever side of the debate you sit on regarding vaccines, a few facts must be clarified. Vaccines have saved millions of lives worldwide. That fact is undeniable. When the pandemic hit, there were tens of thousands of deaths worldwide every day. COVID has killed over 6.5 million people worldwide at the time of writing this book. That number could've been ten times more if it weren't for vaccines. In the UK, at its worst, there were almost two thousand deaths a day. The NHS was on the brink of collapse and healthcare workers were burnout. We all saw the images of NHS staff and healthcare workers globally; their faces bruised and raw from wearing PPE for hours on end. They made us all feel proud to be human. We hailed them as heroes, and they are and will be so forever!

We all stood outside our front doors in the UK on Thursdays during the lockdown and clapped for the NHS. Children put up pictures in windows with rainbows dedicated to the heroes of the NHS. They were the people who did the groundwork that saved millions of lives; they were real-life action heroes. No healthcare system in the world could've prepared for the toll the pandemic would have. Worldwide, it was a reactive process and one that proved the importance of having well-funded healthcare services, not just fit for purpose, but ready for global emergencies. The opposite of what the NHS was when the pandemic hit. A decade of austerity and cuts by a government overrun with dinosaurs and lacking in leadership, critical thinking, and risk management meant the NHS didn't cope. They did what they could with the little they had. Once the vaccinations came into force, they had a dramatic impact on deaths and hospitalisations. There's no doubt that the reason we've been able to get back to any normality post-pandemic is because of vaccinations.

This then presented governments and leaders around the world with the biggest opportunity in modern history; to address our overall health post-lockdown. It provided an opportune moment globally, and as a species. A moment where we could discuss how we can better look after ourselves and those around us with our physical and mental health. Topics such as the importance of diet, exercise, hydration, sleep, meditation, yoga, and breathwork, to name a few, along with the importance of digitally detoxing in the new normal should've been discussed in the mainstream narrative. Similar to how getting vaccinated was important and pushed relentlessly by governments and mainstream media. A few simple health pointers such as these would've gone a long way to empower us as a species to take better care of our health.

Guidance on these matters should've been at the top of the agenda for governments and organisations worldwide. Since illnesses such as cancer, diabetes, obesity, and mental ill health kill millions of people every year around the world. The start of the new normal should have been a global coming together, to mourn our dead and celebrate the battle we were finally winning against Covid. Government guidance on how people and workplaces pick themselves up in the healthiest way should've been the number one priority and step two of the vaccine rollout. This education on health and wellbeing should've been delivered with the same urgency and intensity as vaccines and their rollout. A no-brainer, I'm sure most of you would agree since the job of a government is to always do their best for the electorate.

Unfortunately, that wasn't what happened. Almost immediately, governments and organisations got ahead of themselves and brought in vaccine mandates. The mainstream media did the best they could to pit the vaccinated against the unvaccinated. No matter where you stand on vaccinations, vaccine mandates go against everything we've fought for and stand for in the free world. Once you take choice away from people in a democracy, history has proven the next stage is authoritarianism and dictatorship.

You can see how that process is already underway in the modern world today; in some countries, it's already in place. Even in the UK, civil liberties are being eroded by laws such as the Police, Crime, Sentencing and Courts Act, which take away the right to protest. Laws like these are a blatant attack on freedom and an open door for authoritarian rule. The fact that politicians dare to think and pass such laws is proof of the authoritarian regime we're moving towards, even in the UK.

Authoritarianism is something we all should be opposed to, no matter where you stand on the vaccine issue or on protesting. Let's not forget that protests have changed the course of human history for the better, even though more and more are falling on deaf ears, as people in government assume they know best. From apartheid protests, civil rights protests, Iraq war protests, and women's rights protests to climate change protests, it's been the tool we use to exercise our power as the people. The right to protest is a basic right in a free society, and a tool we've used for generations to tell our governments and leaders when they're getting it wrong. Protests are more important now than ever, as politicians seem to get it wrong, more often than not, these days. Protests have changed brutal laws that people in government have created frequently. From indigenous rights in the USA and Australia, to abolishing slavery. The list goes on and on, so can you imagine what would happen if we lost the right to protest?

No government or organisation "owns" us as humans. They have no right to force or push anyone to get a vaccine. It's not only a breach of the most basic of human rights, but it's a glimpse into an Orwellian nightmare that seems to be unfolding globally. Some governments and employers have concluded they can deal with humans in the same way one might deal with livestock or property. No matter where you stand on the vaccination issue, this should strike a chord with you, we have a humanitarian obligation to stop them in their tracks. If we allow this authoritarian leadership to unfold, there's no telling where it could take us. History has shown us many times over, that this doesn't end well. The worst atrocities in human history have taken place under the rule of authoritarian regimes and dictatorships. One of the last major atrocities led by authoritative rule was the Holocaust, lest we forget!

The democratic process is far from perfect as we learned via Tony Blair and the Iraq war, where a million anti-war protesters were ignored, leading to millions of innocent Iraqi people murdered for non-existent WMDs. We must learn from that history as the consequences go much further than the vaccine issue. No government or organisation should force a human into taking a vaccination, not in a democratic and free society. A person's body is not property, and it's not owned in any shape or form by any institution or government.

Whether a person is for vaccinations, an anti-vaxxer, or anti-vaccine mandate, humans will naturally have differing opinions due to their filters on reality. That's a given; it's simply who we are. Therefore, shutting down any side of the debate is a form of oppression, as there are important conversations to be had on all sides. Shutting down any one side will result in never finding a happy place where healthy conversations and viewpoints can be discussed. Spaces where people can disagree, but still come together for the common good. A lack of this space for dialogue leads to a slanging match rather than a grown-up conversation, thus becoming another tool for polarisation. France and Canada are perfect examples of what happens when one side of a debate is shut down, vilified, and alienated, with complete disregard for what a section of the population feels.

French President Emmanuel Macron vowed to "piss off" those refusing the jab, it beggars belief a president of any country can make such a comment against the people they're supposed to be working for. President Macron passed a law requiring individuals to prove they're fully vaccinated before they can eat out, travel in trains, and attend cultural events which didn't go down well with the French people. Macron then said he wanted to "piss off" unvaccinated people by making their lives so complicated, they'd get jabbed, and that unvaccinated people were irresponsible and unworthy of being considered citizens. This then shut down part of a conversation that France needed to have. This tragic lack of thought on Macron's part lead to protests in Paris as citizens chanted "We'll piss you off." This was not a false threat as protesters from the "convoi de la liberté" blocked the Champs-Élysée and police used tear gas to disperse crowds. The backlash from Macron's comments caused chaos in France. Now, you'd think other world leaders would learn from this situation, but that wasn't the case for Canada's Prime Minister Justin Trudeau.

The trucker-led protests in Canada against vaccine mandates shut down central Ottawa and disrupted cross-border trade. Mr Trudeau slammed the movement as "unacceptable."

He went as far as calling protesters misogynists and racists. Maybe in his individual filter on reality, the movement was "unacceptable," but that's not the view the protestors held. Mr Trudeau's job as PM isn't to tell his citizens what to do and shut them down, but to guide, advise, listen, and find the best way forward. This is a fundamental tenet in leadership, but a fundamental tenet many leaders lack, both in business and politics in modern times. It is evidence that these leaders, don't possess the skill set required for the role they're in. This lack of basic leadership qualities and vision has its consequences for all of us. The consequence for Justin Trudeau was that he had to evacuate to a secret location. In New Zealand, protesters converged on parliament protesting against Jacinda Ardern's decision, who surprisingly and uncharacteristically, showed her lack of empathy and leadership skills by also bringing in vaccine mandates. Similar protests were held in Germany, Austria, Italy, and even Switzerland.

Now, the trucker-led protests in Canada have inspired other countries to stand up for their rights and freedoms with mandates. Canada's aptly named "Freedom Convoy," has given birth to America's aptly named "Peoples Convoy," organised by individuals who believe their freedoms are under threat. What's interesting about the names of these convoys is that they have no mention of vaccines. We're all aware that vaccine mandates sparked them, but the names themselves point to a bigger issue of "people" and their "freedom."

In January 2022 in the U.S., a Texas judge blocked the enforcement of the Joe Biden administration's vaccine mandate for federal workers. What can leaders in politics and organisations learn from this? Both Macron and Trudeau learned the hard way what happens when you disregard, vilify, and push people too far. Macron was voted in for another term in France, not surprising when the other choice was Marine Le Pen. Choosing the lesser of two evils seems to be the political norm in the West, a tragedy for democracy. It brings into question, if these are the only people available in the highly competent West, to do the most important jobs in a country. Looking at the circus of British politics in 2022, with unelected have-a-go Prime Ministers, the disastrous mini-budget that crashed the economy and the British pound, all of which tell us the time has come to rethink the individuals we let run our nations. The same can be said for business leaders in the new normal.

Another interesting fact about the Canadian trucker protests was that most truckers were vaccinated. Canada has one of the highest vaccinated populations in the world, yet both the vaccinated and unvaccinated got behind the protests. Justin Trudeau and mainstream media tried to label the truckers as "anti-vaxxers," but they were simply anti-mandate and pro-freedom. Therefore, organisations all around the world should quickly realise this is bigger than the vaccine issue. These protests are more about civil liberties, human rights, and personal freedoms being eroded by leaders in the free world who have abandoned the fundamental tenets of democracy. It would be just as detrimental for organisations to make the same mistake in the new normal on the vaccine issue.

It's essential to clear up some very basic facts on vaccinations that some are still confused about. The vaccinations don't make a person immune to contracting and spreading COVID. Whether you're vaccinated or not, you can still get COVID, spread it, and die from it. Many double-jabbed people continue to die from COVID every day. Others have died from allergic reactions and other complications encountered from taking the vaccine. Just these facts can naturally make people apprehensive of vaccines, but that is not a reason for them to be alienated, hated or labelled "anti-vaxxers."

When you look at it from this angle, there is no difference between a vaccinated person and an unvaccinated person. What the vaccines do is reduce the risk of a jabbed person dying from COVID. So, a person that doesn't want to get the vaccination is only putting themselves at risk of death, not anyone else. Therefore, an unvaccinated person poses the same level of risk to another person as a vaccinated person. This is a fact many people seem confused about due to misinformation in mainstream media and disinformation on the internet. An unvaccinated person is only a danger to themselves, rather than anyone else.

Some people may think that mandates are necessary, to save those who refuse to get vaccinated, because they're incapable of making the right decision for themselves. Therefore, they should be forced to get the vaccines. If you agree with this viewpoint, then realise that any form of force on civilians is a precursor to dictatorship and dangerous. Others may think we need mandates to ease the pressure on healthcare services. If that was truly the case, why are there no mandates on the sugar and salt we consume in our food? Mandates on the recovery and support given to drug addicts, alcoholics, and those going through mental ill health. All these combined lead to millions of deaths worldwide and puts extreme pressure on healthcare services.

In the UK, many people called the unvaccinated a burden on the NHS. Therefore, to unburden the NHS, they should be vaccinated. The flip side of that argument is, if those people care so much about the burden on the NHS, why aren't they outraged and protesting over the decade of austerity that sucked the soul out of the NHS? As you can see, people will always have differing viewpoints on the same subject, but we must ask why this push for mandates has only happened with vaccines if leadership truly cares about our health? These are all valid questions that the vaccine reluctant are asking, and are relevant questions to ask our leaders, both in the political spectrum and within our workplaces, that are pushing for mandates. We can talk or take sides on the vaccine issue, but this aggressive focus on vaccinations and vaccine mandates brings into question if something else is at play here.

The fact is, billions have been made by a few corporations in big pharma via vaccination rollouts. In the run-up to the development of vaccines, it was clear the first vaccines to market would grab the lion's share of the demand, making billions for the company and its shareholders. In fact, Pfizer made almost $37bn (£27bn) in sales in 2021, making it one of the most lucrative products in history, with forecasted revenues of $98bn to $102bn in 2022. Whether you're a person who believes in the altruism of your government and trusts in big corporations to put people before profit, or if you're a person who believes that government and big corporations are in each other's pockets, and wouldn't trust them as far as you can throw them. Both sides of the argument have a right to be heard and their concerns addressed. That's true democracy and freedom, whether you like it or not.

Whether you trust or distrust your government and big pharma regarding the vaccine issue, we must investigate if there are financial relationships or incentives between big pharma and politicians, that may be causing the push for vaccine mandates. If there are financial benefits, how does that influence the approval process for vaccinations and the decision-making process of world leaders pushing for mandates? Are mandates really about healthcare? Are they a misguided political perception or something more sinister? These are all relevant questions that the vaccine reluctant have, based on their window on the world. Questions that need and deserve answers.

The fact is, there is big money and big profits with COVID vaccinations. The Pfizer/BioNTech vaccine, now known as Comirnaty, will be one of the most lucrative drugs in pharmaceutical history. Tom Frieden, the former senior U.S. health official, accused Pfizer of "war profiteering" during the pandemic. Ministers in the UK have agreed to a secrecy clause in any disputes with Pfizer regarding the UK's vaccine supply. Large portions of government contracts have been redacted and any arbitration proceedings are kept secret. Now, why would the UK agree to something so ridiculous when talking about public health paid for via the public purse? In fact, how can any government hide any financial dealings when all the money comes from taxpayers ultimately? Authoritarianism? Corruption? Or both?

Regarding this, Zain Rizvi, the research director at Public Citizen, a U.S. consumer advocacy organisation, said: "There's a wall of secrecy surrounding these contracts, and it's unacceptable, particularly in a public health crisis." Rizvi brought up the necessity for the UK government to explain why the UK agreed that arbitration proceedings could be handled secretly. The UK was the only high-income country that agreed to such a provision, allowing pharmaceutical companies to circumnavigate Britain's domestic legal process. Rizvi went on to say, "The UK government has allowed the drug firms to call the shots. How did we end up in a situation where a handful of drug firms exerted so much control over the most powerful governments in the world? It points to a broken system."

These are real and valid concerns, and big pharma has an eye-opening history of fraud and underhanded tactics. If we take Pfizer, for example, in 1986, Pfizer withdrew an artificial heart valve from the market due to defects leading to over three hundred deaths. In 2003, Pfizer was accused of profiteering from AIDS drugs after Pfizer walked away from a licensing deal that would have made AIDS drugs cheaper for poorer countries. In 2011, Pfizer paid compensation to families of children killed in Trovan drug trials. When the meningitis epidemic hit Africa in 1996, Pfizer ran trials of Trovan in Nigeria, which killed eleven children out of two hundred. It caused liver damage and lifelong disabilities in the survivors.

In 2012, Pfizer paid $1 billion to settle lawsuits because of the claims that its Prempro drug caused breast cancer. They used Prempro in hormone replacement therapy, most of the time for women going through menopause. It took six years for the settlement to be paid because of Pfizer fighting the case. In 2013, Pfizer paid $273 million to settle over 2,000 cases against them in the U.S. over their drug Chantix. Chantix was a smoking treatment, but users claimed it lead to self-harm, suicidal ideation, homicidal ideation, and severe psychological disorders. Alarmingly, Pfizer was accused of improperly excluding patients with mental health issues such as depression or other mental disturbances from the drug trials. In 2017, a coroner in Australia ruled that Chantix contributed to the suicide of a man. As recent as 2020, Pfizer settled with thousands of customers over its depo-testosterone drug after being sued because the drug increases the likelihood of heart attack and many other issues.

When we look at this type of information, it's no wonder millions of people are vaccine reluctant. It brings into question for some people and rightly so, how safe vaccines are. If they've been brought to market in a rush for profit, rather than going through the stringent checks required to approve vaccinations to the masses. It begs the question of how many vaccinated people wouldn't have had the jab, if they were aware of this information. It also questions how many people got jabbed because they felt bullied, pressured, or felt like they had no choice by their employer and the government. I need to clarify that I'm not singling Pfizer out, they're just a good example of why someone may be vaccine reluctant. Knowing this information, it could be considered that all those who rushed off to get vaccinated and those pushing the unvaccinated to get jabs, are the ones that lack critical thinking, and not the vaccine-reluctant "conspiracy theorists."

When it comes to any form of pharmaceutical drug, there is a risk and benefit scale. Even though we may not like to hear this, some people will die due to taking vaccines and medications. It's part and parcel, therefore, having concerns about the vaccines and the corporations that created them is rational and valid. It would be naïve to think that pharmaceutical companies aren't profit-driven, they are, which does lead to corruption. In 2009, Pfizer settled the biggest criminal fine in US history as part of a $2.3bn settlement for misbranding the painkiller Bextra, due to promoting the drug for uses that were not approved by medical regulators and paying kickbacks to compliant doctors. This settlement was a part of a lawsuit by whistle-blower John Kopchinski, a Pfizer sales rep in Florida. Kopchinksi quoted "At Pfizer, I was expected to increase profits at all costs, even when sales meant endangering lives. I couldn't do that,"

This all happened while not under any emergency provisions or time factors, as was the case for COVID vaccines. For the vaccine reluctant, this is an alarming thought. Revelations of poor practices at Ventavia, a contracted research company carrying out Pfizer's pivotal COVID-19 vaccine trials, raised questions about data integrity and regulatory oversight. Brook Jackson, a regional director at Ventavia Research Group, claimed the company falsified data, unblinded patients, and employed vaccinators with inadequate training. Jackson claimed staff were overwhelmed by the number of problems in the phase 3 trials. Fed up with Ventavia's inaction, Jackson emailed the FDA in a cry for help, and she was fired the same day.

In a recorded meeting in September 2020 between Jackson and two Ventavia directors, an executive is heard saying the company couldn't quantify the types and numbers of errors in the trials regarding quality control. The executive was recorded saying, "In my mind, it's something new every day," and, "We know that it's significant." Just two months later, in November 2020, Pfizer announced data from Phase 3 clinical trials showing the vaccine was safe and effective, with an efficacy of 95%. Many people who are reluctant to get their jabs are concerned with how quickly the vaccine was developed and how diligent that process was. These events highlight that these fears weren't unfounded.

According to the International Federation of Pharmaceutical Manufacturers & Associations (IFPMA), the development of vaccines usually takes between ten to fifteen years. This is due to the time needed in clinical trials for establishing its quality, safety, and efficacy over time and to meet regulatory requirements. The COVID vaccines were developed in under a year and were approved by healthcare regulatory bodies such as the Department of Health and Social Care here in the UK and the CDC and FDA in America. We were told the reason the vaccines were approved so quickly was because of the unlimited funding, resources, and new technology available to speed up the process of research and development of the vaccines. However, no amount of funding and resources can speed up the process regarding any complications that may possibly show up over time. No doctor or scientist can claim these vaccines won't cause health complications due to the lack of long-term clinical data. This, for many, is a valid and rational cause for concern because if there's a risk, there must be a choice, not mandates in a free society. Dr Robert Malone eloquently put this in Defeat the Mandates Rally in Washington D.C. He said, "If there is risk there must be a choice, all medical procedures and drugs have risks. All of us have the right to understand these risks and decide for ourselves if we are willing to accept those risks. To deny this is to deny human dignity."

Now it's clear we didn't have ten to fifteen years to develop the COVID vaccine. We had to "rush it through" to save millions of lives. The emergency use approval process, regulation 174 of the Human Medicine Regulations 2012, enables rapid temporary regulatory approvals to address significant public health issues, such as a pandemic. The fact is, we were stuck between a rock and a hard place. As much as it doesn't sit well with many, it can be considered the right decision to rush through these approvals as safely as possible and get them to the mass market. At this point, I need to clarify that I'm not trying to scare vaccinated people with the information I'm listing in this chapter. I just want to level the playing field between the vaccinated being right, responsible and level-headed citizens and the unvaccinated being selfish conspiracy theorists and worthless citizens!

There are valid reasons to be vaccinated and valid reasons to be unvaccinated. Hopefully, there won't be any health implications in the future due to vaccines. In that scenario, companies like Pfizer can be held accountable for saving billions of lives and, in my opinion, should be hailed as heroes. Pharmaceutical companies have saved billions of lives historically and continue to do so daily. However, a Texas judge overruled a request by the FDA in 2022 to take until 2097 to release the data it relied on to license Pfizer's COVID-19 vaccine. Why would the FDA want to wait until everyone who got vaccinations died from old age, before releasing this information to the public?

The judge ruled that complete documentation must be in the public domain by the end of summer 2022, rather than the seventy-five years requested by the FDA. This kind of development does no favours for both the FDA and Pfizer. It only leads to more people becoming vaccine-hesitant, and fuels the anti-vax school of thought, and mistrust of the government and big pharma. These documents are now being released and insightfully broken down and presented by Dr John Campbell on his channel on YouTube.

The information I've presented in this chapter shows that vaccine-hesitant people are simply humans, with real and relevant questions and concerns that all leadership has a duty of care to address. Now let's consider the current situation of the UK's beloved NHS. The NHS has been understaffed and underfunded for a decade, yet these real-life heroes stood up with the little they had, did what they could, and saved millions of lives. Due to the vaccine mandates coming into force in the NHS, a lot of those same "heroes" left. The NHS was told that all healthcare workers needed to be fully vaccinated or be dismissed at a time the NHS desperately needs skills and a larger workforce. That means those same people we clapped for on Thursdays during the lockdown, the same people we hailed as heroes, the same people who saved millions of lives, under torturous physical and mental burnout-inducing conditions during the pandemic; those same people who worked risking their own lives unvaccinated, are no longer welcome in the NHS due to being unvaccinated. Talk about cutting off your nose to spite your face!

Thankfully, the UK government came to its senses and launched a consultation on revoking the vaccination mandate for health and care staff in England. Sajid Javid, the then incumbent UK's Secretary of State, was pushing for vaccine mandates for the NHS and was confronted by Dr Steve James at the Kings College Hospital London. In a video that went viral, Mr Javid asked a group of nurses what they thought of the requirement for vaccine mandates. He was met with an awkward silence. Dr Steve James then jumped in to tell Mr Javid he had worked through the entire pandemic, had contracted covid, and had his natural antibodies, which are more effective than vaccines. Dr James told Mr Javid he wasn't vaccinated and didn't want to be. Why should he have to be dismissed? Dr Steve James told Mr Javid that the science is not strong enough to bring in vaccine mandates. Mr Javid announced in February 2022 that it was "no longer proportionate" to make the jabs compulsory and made a U-turn on vaccine mandates for NHS staff.

In the new normal, employers can learn much from the mistakes made at a political level, instead of being influenced by them. Organisations mandating vaccines will face similar uprisings and will exacerbate the great resignation, organisations must weigh up the necessity of vaccine mandates in the new normal. They need to evaluate if mandates are proportionate to the negatives of implementing such requirements for employees. The adult social care sector in the UK lost forty thousand staff as a result of compulsory vaccinations. Mike Padgham the chair of the Independent Care Group, explained: "We warned many good, kind and caring professional staff would be lost to the policy and that proved to be the case. Most of those we will never get back."

For an organisation, the vaccination issue is kindred to the race issue. The best person for the job may be a PGM, just like the best person for the job may be unvaccinated. Organisations need to consider if vaccine mandates are the best policy in line with their recruitment needs, and ability to attract the best talent. Do organisations want to be viewed as employers that forced their employees to get vaccines in breach of human and democratic freedoms? Or should organisations keep within the essential boundaries of our free society and seek to protect their employees and themselves via a different approach?

There are many reasons an employer may consider vaccine mandates. Initially, vaccine mandates can appear as the only solution to the vaccine issue. Therefore, they can come about as a knee-jerk reaction. A quick fix for COVID. However, we know now that millions of people are vaccine reluctant, and they have every right to be so. Therefore, organisations in the new normal should give employees freedom of choice with vaccines. They should create legal documents that spell out the dangers of being unvaccinated at work, and write off any liabilities as an employer, with transmission and death in the workplace. This is the best way forward for employers and employees. An unvaccinated person fully understands the implications and risks they run both at work, and in their personal lives, regarding their choice not to be vaccinated. Therefore, it's not unfair for an employer to mitigate any legal issues with an unvaccinated employee via their contract of employment.

When you look at the policy of vaccine mandates, they're simply someone else's viewpoint being forced on other people. Mandates can be considered a "quick fix" and profit-driven with total disregard for personal freedoms. Mandates can be considered a product of a decision made by one set of people wanting to be right, rather than hearing and considering the concerns of another set of people. Vaccine mandates have no place in the working world in the new normal. Mandates only show a lack of critical thinking in leaders and the inability to find solutions to new-age challenges. Any organisation considering vaccine mandates should realise this is far more than a vaccine/COVID issue. It is about democracy, personal freedoms, and civil liberties. Organisational decisions that erode these most basic of human rights, will have to face the consequences of those decisions. When it comes to the vaccine issue, organisations should be careful not to cut off their nose, to spite their face!

7

The Gender Issue

The gender issue at work is an area that organisations have been trying to resolve and find a happy place with for generations. In this chapter, I'll avoid going down the path of well-known gender issues at work, such as pay gaps, sexual harassment, and disparities in females present in CEO and senior management roles. These issues have been covered in much detail over the years by many writers and leaders, they are still completely relevant in the new normal. There's still much work to be done by employers regarding these gender issues, even though progress has been made because of awareness raised over the last few years.

In this chapter, I wanted to touch on lesser established and discussed gender issues that are just as important and shed some light on what employers and managers can do, to raise awareness, in order to become more literate on their management in the new normal. Gender, in the traditional sense, is regarded as either of the two sexes, male or female.

However, the meaning of gender, according to the Oxford English Dictionary, is:

Either of the two sexes (male and female), especially when considered with reference to social and cultural differences rather than biological ones. The term is also used more broadly to denote a range of identities that do not correspond to established ideas of male and female. "A condition that affects people of both genders."

As with mental health and wellbeing at work, the new normal is a time to refocus and rethink the gender issue at work to find some real-world solutions. Hybrid working in some respects has had a positive impact on the gender issue. A survey by Aviva, a British multinational insurance company, found more men wanted to return to the office than women, who preferred working from home. This may be due to more women traditionally having primary care roles with their children. Hybrid working has helped share the burden of childcare for women, with men now taking more of a role in the care of their children during the working week.

Gender Issue

In one of my training courses, a male learner told the group he had never taken his son to school until hybrid working came into play. Due to work, he had to leave early, and the kids were back home from school by the time he got home from work. Since hybrid working, he was able to take his son to school for the first time, meet other parents on the school run and get to know his son's school friends. He said he never had the opportunity to be involved with that part of his son's life and realised how important it was as a father. He felt he had missed out because of his job and stated he loved taking his son to school, and spending that quality time made his mornings. His wife loved it as she got an extra bit of sleep in the morning, which gave her a much-needed respite from duties that had always been hers. He was used to spending his mornings sitting in traffic, stressing and hoping there were no accidents or roadworks. That's how he had spent his mornings for years. This is a small example of how hybrid working can positively affect a person's day and family life. In this case, it had a positive on him and his wife.

Hybrid working is something that organisations should seek to leverage for better management of people. One way to leverage this opportunity in the new normal is for employers to introduce staggered start and finish times for employees, where possible. Traditionally, the hours between 7 a.m. and 9 a.m. are the most stressful times of the day for most workers. Many workers with families need to get themselves ready, get their children ready, get them to school, and get themselves into work all by 9 a.m. They're up against rush hour traffic jams, packed trains and buses, and the fear that if anything goes wrong in the delicate balancing act, the result would mean arriving late for work. As a Londoner, I found these hours to be the most stressful times of my working week. I moved nearer to my place of work, rather than start my day like that five days a week. Staggering start and finish times to ease the burden on employees during these stress-filled hours of the day, will go a long way toward the wellbeing of employees in the new normal.

Many people don't have the luxury of moving closer to work due to owning the house they live in. They cannot uproot their children from their schools and move away from friends and family support in the area they live. I experienced this first-hand growing up, witnessing the work rate of my mother and father. They worked like slaves from the moment they stepped foot into the UK as immigrants, until the day they retired. An experience played out for generations within working-class families and is still being played out today. Unfortunately, this living-to-work lifestyle comes with social issues and consequences for society.

This unhealthy start to the day usually results in an unhealthy end to the day. Workers must go through the same rigmarole they do in the morning, trying to get back home through rush hour traffic and packed public transport in the evening. Londoners especially will know what that "rush hour hell" feels like, especially on the way to and from work using the Tube. One in fourteen people has anxiety about taking the Tube in London. A survey conducted of over 5,500 commuters in London, Rome, Barcelona, Berlin, Madrid, and Paris, found that the stress of the commute was on par with a relationship breakdown. That's a stress impact equivalent to two relationship breakdowns a day, five days a week. That's a lot of stress to be dealing with just to go back and forth from work. Two-thirds of Londoners said public transport was the most stressful part of living in the city, the Tube being the worst of the lot.

There's no let-up for drivers either. Research by Robins and Day, a Peugeot-owned car dealership, found that 44% of motorists said 5 p.m. to 7 p.m. was the most stressful part of the day and 32% said 7 a.m. to 9 a.m. was when they were most on edge. As you can see, many employees in the UK, and much likely worldwide, are frazzled from the morning commute, then frazzled again from the evening commute. This unhealthy pattern of stress will undoubtedly affect a person's mental health, affecting both their personal and professional lives. Many people view a stressful commute as a fact of life, something we cannot change and must accept and get on with. This, however, need not be the case in the new normal. Employers have a huge opportunity to make a major impact on employee stress levels. Employers must act to leverage this opportunity in the new normal and reap the benefits of a less stressed-out workforce.

Any person being under that much stress, day in and day out, is unhealthy. This is all before they deal with stress at work. Stress is a major contributor to mental and physical health issues; it affects how we feel generally about life and how we lead our lives. Many spend their working week too exhausted to deal with anything else other than work. This is the perfect example of what's meant by living to work. Many people pay for after-school clubs and ask family and friends to help pick up their children from school and babysit. This type of working day usually means that people are exhausted by the end of each day. The consequence is millions of families not getting the time to nurture and enjoy the most important parts of life. Their family life, health, social life, and downtime.

For many, this leads to the need for escapism, and the thought of some freedom as the weekend approaches is exciting. Fun in the West is usually linked to alcohol, substances, or both. In the West, alcohol and substance use have become our go-to in order to escape our reality. When you look at the data, it can be considered, people are addicted to drugs as much as they are addicted to escaping the reality of life. Alcohol and drug misuse can be conquered, but how can we conquer a reality we're not fully in charge of, or happy with? Perhaps there's a realisation that there's no drug in the world that can make life meaningful. Perhaps that realisation is one reason contributing to the great resignation. People want better.

Gender, Substance Misuse and Suicide

Many view this form of escapism as culture and "what we do." However, most people don't realise it can also be a dependency and a coping strategy linked to unhappiness, personality disorders, and mental health issues. As the weekend approaches, many binge drink to cope with the stress of the working week and life in general, unaware they're using these substances as a coping mechanism. Due to how alcohol is embedded in British culture, and in the West. With alcohol being omnipresent in every aspect of our lives, we can perceive alcohol as a friend, thus linking it to fun, unaware of the damage it does. According to data by Statista, a New York-based business data platform found that the UK spent £26 Billion on alcohol in 2020, which was a rise of £5 Billion from 2019. It begs the question does the UK have a major drinking problem we need to confront?

According to Drinkaware, 27% of people binge drink each week on their heaviest drinking day in the UK, with 28% of men and 25% of women binge drinking. For substances, forensic scientists at King's College London studied wastewater in London looking for benzoylecgonine (BE), a compound produced by the human body when breaking down cocaine. They found London consumed 23kgs of cocaine daily. That was higher than Barcelona, Berlin, and Amsterdam combined. Worryingly, these are the next three highest consumers of cocaine in Europe. The street value of 23kgs of cocaine in the UK is around £12 million. That's £12 million of cocaine going up people's noses every day just in London.

We do have a massive issue with drink and drugs in the UK. Frighteningly this is data for just two substances: alcohol and cocaine. Employers in the new normal can't ignore the impact of drink and drug use. It has a huge impact on working life, with many consuming whilst at work. Substance misuse is so widespread in the UK, that traces of cocaine have been found in eleven out of twelve toilets in Parliament. Toilets only accessible to MPs, lawmakers, staffers, and journalists. This included a toilet closest to British Prime Minister Boris Johnson's office. If there's drug use in the UK parliament, employers shouldn't rule out the fact that it's happening within their organisations. Some employers and managers know, yet turn a blind eye. Employers shouldn't bury their heads in the sand with this issue. Employers will need to accept it for what it is and address the issue appropriately. This isn't about having a zero-tolerance policy. That's never worked, and it never will. It's more about education and training that highlights and raises awareness of the reasons people use substances, and the detrimental impact it has on a person's life.

There are many other forms of substances with drugs such as ketamine and "balloons," which is Nitrous Oxide, in heavy use in the UK. Nitrous Oxide is a dissociative drug usually inhaled from a balloon and delivered via small gas canisters, a drug issue running rampant amongst the young. Dissociative drugs distort the perception of sight and sound and produce feelings of detachment. At Notting Hill Carnival in 2022, 3.5 tonnes of empty gas canisters were cleared up filling four skips. Then there's skunk weed, which probably has the widest use of any other drug, and increases your risk of serious mental illness.

Research conducted by Lancet Psychiatry estimates around one in ten new cases of psychosis is possibly associated with skunk cannabis. In London and Amsterdam, where most of the very strong skunk cannabis is sold, it's higher. An average of 21% of new cases of psychosis are associated with daily cannabis use and nearly a third with high-potency skunk cannabis. Skunk contains more Tetrahydrocannabinol (THC) than regular cannabis. THC can induce psychotic symptoms, such as hallucinations, delusions, and paranoia. Researchers at King's College London found the skunk variant of the plant damaged the corpus callosum, the part of the brain which carries signals between the brain's left and right sides. From this data, it's clear as a nation, we're no longer saying no to drugs. We're saying yes to drugs like never before.

Combine that with the consumption of prescription drugs for mental health issues, which, according to the NHS makes up 79.4 million antidepressant drugs prescribed to 7.87 million patients in 2020/21. That's one in every eight people in the UK. Anti-depressant use amongst young people is the highest ever on record. That's the same for the adult population, with half of all adults in the UK on antidepressants. An organisation unaware of how many employees are currently on prescription medication can't hope to manage them effectively. The number of antidepressants issued and the number of patients receiving antidepressant drugs increased for the fifth consecutive year.

Addiction Center, a U.S.-based addiction and recovery guide, found that more men than women abuse illicit drugs and alcohol. Roughly, 11.5% of men and boys over the age of twelve have a substance use disorder, compared to 6.4% of women and girls. More women, however, go to the hospital because of substance abuse or fatally overdosing. Women are also more likely to develop a dependency on lower drinking levels. In the UK, according to Statista, deaths due to drug misuse by gender have been rising since 1993. In 1993, 577 men died from drug misuse, for women it was 254. By 2020, this number had increased to 2,165 for men and 800 for women per year. The use of anti-depressants doubled from 2008 to 2018 before the pandemic. In 2008, there were 36 million anti-depressants prescribed. By 2018, the number was 70.9 million. A record high has been set for women prescribed antidepressants since the beginning of the pandemic. According to the United Nations, 269 million people used drugs worldwide in 2018, that's 30% more than in 2009.

Now, some industries don't have the luxury of a hybrid working option, and workers must be present. Construction is one of those. The male-dominated construction industry has a huge problem with alcohol and substance misuse and is the perfect example of why employers must take this matter seriously in the new normal. In a study of over 1,300 construction workers, the Considerate Constructors Scheme, a not-for-profit founded to raise standards in the construction industry, found that 35% of construction workers found colleagues to be under the influence of either alcohol or drugs while on the job.

It isn't surprising that the construction industry has the highest rate of suicide of any profession in the UK. The gender and substance misuse issue in construction is an obvious one, with fathers, husbands, sons, brothers, and uncles killing themselves at a rate of ten people per week in construction in the UK. It's a national tragedy, and it will require government intervention and the extinction of many dinosaurs in the construction sector and at the Health and Safety Executive (HSE) to fix this issue. The rules, regulations, and heavy fines set by the HSE have resulted in construction companies protecting themselves over the needs of their workers, creating a toxic employer Vs. employee culture in the construction sector.

It's created a tick-box culture where construction companies use health and safety regulations to protect themselves over and against their workers. This has resulted in construction workers becoming an easily disposable asset and being treated in such a manner. The industry is riddled with rogue site supervisors and managers who tip off workers when the drug testers are due. Accidents because of health and safety breaches can be handled via paid time off, and as a payoff, for not reporting it to avoid heavy fines for dangerous working conditions and costly HSE investigations. This is the tip of the iceberg when it comes to problematic working conditions in the construction sector. I've received this information directly from construction workers in my training courses, including site supervisors and managers. As many say, "it's just the way things are!"

The HSE needs to accept that its rules and regulations are being manipulated in the real world, thus perpetuating this horrific situation in the construction industry. The new normal is a time for a rethink with new people and new ideas in construction. The construction sector is a harsh warning to employers of what can happen when mental health, wellbeing, better standards for managing people, and awareness of substance misuse are ignored in the workplace. It's a look down a rabbit hole that highlights why employers in every other sector, must do everything they can, to avoid a similar situation.

On gender and suicide, there's a narrative that men are three times more likely to kill themselves compared to women. This is only true if you look at deaths by suicide. A cross-national study on gender differences in suicide intent by BMC Psychiatry, an open-access, peer-reviewed journal, found that men have disproportionately lower rates of suicide attempts but excessively higher rates of deaths by suicide compared to women. This is called the gender paradox of suicidal behaviour.

Studies have found that the intent for women to die from suicide is lower and the methods used are less lethal compared to men. Men use more violent and lethal methods of suicide, and that's the only reason men have a suicide rate three times higher than women. Women are more likely to self-harm and major depression is twice as likely in women than men. Both of which contribute to suicidal ideation and behaviour. Therefore, suicide is an all-gender issue. Unfortunately, the entire mental health community in the UK pushes this narrative that men are three times more likely to kill themselves than women, thus having more of a problem with suicide. This is a misleading narrative, and a dangerous one.

This misleading narrative on men has given rise to toxic labels and terminology such as "toxic masculinity." This is a term I detest, and one used to perpetuate this misleading narrative on men and suicide. The term itself can read like masculinity is toxic, which is also false and dangerous. A healthy perception of masculinity is needed for the wellbeing of men today, so labelling any part of masculinity as toxic can be damaging. For me, there's no such thing as toxic masculinity, just a toxic society where men feel unable to express their thoughts and feelings safely. This is because of the fear of being perceived as weak or a lesser man by others. It's also linked to what women may think of them if they opened up and showed vulnerability. This is a societal issue, not a masculine one.

Now, a lot of guys I've spoken with in my courses and in general life think, "Here we go again," when it comes to men and mental health. A lot of men think this is where everyone tells them to open up, talk more, get more in touch with their emotions, and even cry because "toxic masculinity" is bad for them. This approach to mental health may work for some men. However, I've found a lot of men are bored with this narrative, which has become a cause for further disengagement with mental health. What I've learned during my work as an MHFA instructor and from being involved in men's groups myself, is that men require the correct masculine environment to open, discuss, and express emotions and thoughts.

This is why men find it much easier to open up in men's groups. I've witnessed this many times in men's groups I've been involved with, and men have a lot to say about how they feel. They just need the correct masculine environment to do so. Men need a purpose and it's important to learn about things to avoid and things to do to keep healthy. In this way, men can be there for those they love, as men have a natural need to protect who and what they love. Employers need to be mindful of men's mental health issues and perceptions, especially in a male-dominated workforce. The biggest killer of men forty-five years and under is suicide, and we know men aged 40–50 years old have the highest rate of suicide of any demographic in the UK.

On the flip side of that, suicide is the biggest killer of 5–19-year-olds. Female teenage suicides are the highest ever on record. The biggest killer of us all, thirty-five years old and under, is suicide. Therefore, I encourage every single organisation in the mental health sector in the UK, to readdress this misleading narrative, and educate the public on the truth regarding suicide. I encourage them to do it quickly. If we overly focus on men with suicide, we circumnavigate the truth about women and the young regarding suicide. If we keep pushing this misleading narrative on men, it could be women killing themselves at three times the rate of men in the future. We must be careful with that. Women already have the gender issue stacked against them; let's avoid creating another challenge for women to overcome in the new normal.

Not surprisingly, 30–50% of people with severe mental illness also have problems with alcohol and substance misuse. This is called a dual diagnosis in mental health. This isn't just a UK issue, even though we seem to be the most addicted and dependent in Europe. Alcohol and substance misuse are rife in a lot of major cities in the West, and we need to ask ourselves why. Here in the UK, we have a major drink and drug problem. Employers must be literate on this issue for better people management in the new normal.

According to the Journal of the American Medical Association, 50% of people with severe mental disorders are affected by substance abuse in the U.S. On top of that, 37% of alcohol abusers and 53% of drug abusers also have at least one serious mental health issue. In America, of all people diagnosed with a mental illness, 29% misuse alcohol or drugs. Drinking and drug use have a huge impact on mental health and wellbeing, which has a major impact on a person's working life. Thankfully, this is a topic covered in MHFA training, giving an employer a good foundation and starting point to raise awareness on the matter, and set up frameworks to support and raise awareness in the workplace.

Gender and Hybrid Working

With hybrid working, we have an opportunity to massively reduced traditional stressors for employees during the working week. It's important to remember that any positive impact on the working week that reduces stress can help to curtail the need for the "weekend blowout," and dependency on substances and other unhelpful coping strategies. This is a culture rabid and rampant, and one that must be dismantled for healthier and happier people and workforce. Organisations making a serious effort with hybrid working to reduce stress won't only be contributing to mental wellbeing in their workforce, but also to society. I cannot think of a better form of self-regulation for an organisation's corporate social responsibility.

Well managed hybrid working should mean a person works from home at least 3 days a week. For two fixed days (Tuesday and Wednesday) everyone should be in the office. This helps to address the all-important human-to-human contact and cuts down on emails and other forms of digital communication. The flexibility of coming to work for more than two days a week should be available for those that need the interaction. This immediately reduces more than 50% of the travelling stress for an employee. A significant drop in stress levels. This opportunity to make such a large dent in employee stress levels wasn't an option pre-pandemic, it's a gift of the new normal, and employers should take full advantage. This reduction in stress is a huge leap forward for employee wellbeing, and if managed well, it can have minimal impact on operations.

Implemented well, opportunities like staggered working hours will have a small impact on the employer but a large positive impact on the employee. For an employee, it will have a positive impact on their wellbeing and their work-life balance, making them happier and more productive. Employers shouldn't underestimate the benefits of small tweaks like this in the working day. It can mean the difference between an employee staying with an organisation for ten years rather than a year, the difference between slow and rapid growth, and the difference between a healthy or toxic workplace culture. Employers must decide now, how they want their future to look in the new normal.

In the new normal, employees will need to feel that an organisation understands their reality. Staggered working hours give an employer the perfect opportunity to show they do. Staff retention is a top priority for organisations post-pandemic. Every positive tweak helps. Hybrid working is the future and should be exploited for managing people in the new normal. The future of work is all about finding a "win-win" or "happy place" for both employer and employee at every given opportunity. Organisations looking to do away with hybrid working should think twice. Hybrid working future-proofs organisations against another pandemic or global emergency that will surely come. Doing away with it is the same as chasing your tail, a good thing if you like going around in circles. It's a no-brainer for hybrid working to be the norm in the new normal. Those organisations seeking to do away with hybrid working are led by dinosaurs that lack vision and are a hindrance to organisational stability in the new normal. Best practice in how to manage people in the new hybrid working environment, needs to be an area of people management, organisations and HR should explore and exploit.

Hybrid working must be embraced and leveraged in the new normal. It's a surprise gift that's materialised post-pandemic, helping employees to secure a healthier work and life balance. The freedom to work in our pyjamas now and again, get more sleep, reduce travel stress, save money on travel and food costs, and get more family time is a huge positive shift in the working world. One of several positive things to materialise from the pandemic. Hybrid working also provides an opportunity to focus on female employees, levelling up the traditional childcare roles within the family unit. It also helps to better manage and support, the natural biological processes female employees undergo, throughout their working life.

Leveraging hybrid working will contribute to creating workplaces where employees stay long-term, or for life, like a lot of our parents did. It can help reverse the trend of the great resignation. For female employees, the new normal also provides an opportunity to have a second look at gender disparities and challenges faced by women in the workplace. In recent years, gender disparities in the pay gap and women in senior management positions have improved. Nevertheless, there are certain challenges women face that aren't so mainstream or haven't received the attention it requires. Challenges essential for employers and managers to conquer in the new normal.

Pregnancy

Pregnancy and mental health are an area employers must refocus on for better management of female staff during and post-pregnancy. There's a lot more to pregnancy than most employers and people realise, all of which affects a woman's mental health and workplace performance. When a woman becomes pregnant, it's usually such a joyous event we forget the mental and physical toll it can take.

At the end of the pregnancy, a woman pushes a fully functioning human out into the world. It's not a walk in the park.

The impact of pregnancy became clearer during my daughter's pregnancy and the birth of my granddaughter, than it did when my daughter was born. My daughter's labour was traumatic, which led to some mental health complications post-birth. When a baby is born, it's a cause for celebration. Often the mother being joyous, and well, is taken as a given. I learned this isn't always the case through the experience of my daughter's pregnancy. My daughter was in surgery for several hours after giving birth and was a zombie when she came out of surgery due to being heavily sedated. She spent seven days in the hospital before she was able to stand and come home with the baby.

My Father with my daughter Sarisha and my granddaughter Shaiya, a few days after the hospital discharge.

Many of us have heard of the term "the baby blues," but how many managers and CEOs truly realise what it means? How many managers are aware of the mental health implications when a woman becomes pregnant, especially if the manager is male or a female manager that isn't a mother? As a CEO and as a man, I'll be the first to put my hands up and say I wasn't well versed in the implications and complications of pregnancy, the time of the month, menopause, and other natural processes a woman and a woman's body must deal with during a lifetime. As a CEO or a manager, especially if you're a man, it's impossible to manage female employees competently without being literate on these matters.

I feel embarrassed to say I was not literate on these matters in my last role as a CEO, even though 98% of my staff were women and my entire management team was female. This is why being a great CEO, leader, or manager, is a journey of continual learning, and not a destination. If you're a male CEO or manager, ask yourself how well-versed you are in these matters. I can take a wild guess and say most male CEOs and managers don't have a clue about the true impact of these natural biological processes on women, and how it affects mental health and working life. During and post-pregnancy, female employees can develop a host of mental health issues, including anxiety and depression, post-partum psychosis, PTSD, and schizophrenia. One in five women develop mental health issues during pregnancy or after giving birth. Pregnancy can exacerbate existing mental health issues, with depression and anxiety being the most common affecting fifteen out of every hundred women. If you are a CEO or a manager, were you aware of this?

Research from King's College London found that pregnant women with serious mental illnesses are at a higher risk of renal failure, heart attacks, and embolisms during childbirth. This data is proof of why it's vital for employers, CEOs, and managers to be trained and literate on the complexities of pregnancy. It needs as much attention as gender pay gaps and the lack of women holding senior positions in business. To address the disproportionate role women play in childcare, and to ease the burden of potential complications, employers must also consider fathers. True parity can only be had, when fathers can take time off to be with their newborns, and support their partners, during this fragile time. Some employers, such as John Lewis, have set the benchmark with this and offer equal pay and leave for both parents during this vulnerable time. In the new normal, this should be the standard for all employers.

This goes hand in hand with the management of female employees and awareness regarding menstruation. For far too long, women have been mocked for showing emotion or irritability in society at their time of the month. It's also crept into the working world. I've even heard women mock other women using derogative language regarding menstruation many times as a CEO. "Careful, I think she's on her period today," or "calm down, are you on your period or something?" I'm sure every reader can relate to this. It happens in the workplace, in our homes, and in social circles. Coming from a family of women and having been a CEO in a female-dominated workplace, I can safely say I've been on the receiving end of that irritability, both growing up and in the working world, which I understood and made space for.

Women on their periods can experience excruciating pain, heavy bleeding, and painful cramps. On the flip side of that, some lucky women have periods that have little impact on their lives but even that can change from month to month. When it comes to Aunty Flo, you cannot predict how irritable or what mood she will be in, month in and month out. Therefore, employers and managers should expect irritability and a drop in performance from female employees during this time and make concessions for it. A poll of 3,000 workers by the charity Bloody Good Period found that, nine out of ten women experienced stress or anxiety in the workplace because of their periods. The poll also uncovered a lack of trust, confidence, proactivity and leadership in UK workplaces regarding menstruation.

Looking back, I may have subconsciously concluded that since my entire management team were female, somehow, these matters would be dealt with by my all-female management team. Luckily for me, they were, even though as a management team, we never spoke or trained on the management challenges linked to female biological processes. How many readers of this book, no matter what your position at work, can say you have been adequately trained by your employer, and are literate, on the management of menstruation?

In my organisation, this lack of awareness didn't lead to any issues because of the female-dominated staff base. My management team was confident in guiding me to what needed to be done on such matters. As a male CEO or manager, it can be uncomfortable speaking to a female member of staff on such matters and vice versa. A lot of male CEOs and managers may have come to the same conclusion, basically leaving female employees to sort out female matters. This is understandable to a point, as some female employees will only want to speak to another female employee. This, however, can only work if there's a good balance between female and male employees in management positions. Another great reason for both male and female representation to be equal in a management hierarchy. That doesn't mean, however, that these matters are no longer on a male CEO or manager's remit. In the new normal, it should be an essential part of management training regardless of gender. In a male-dominated work environment, a lack of female representation could leave a female member of staff feeling isolated and vulnerable at a time they require support from their manager.

According to the World Economic Forum, 2022 saw a record for female CEOs in America's Fortune 500 companies, a positive step forward. Yet that's still only 15% female representation at the top of America's biggest public companies. At the CEO level, men outnumber women seventeen to one, and female CEOs are more likely to be fired than male CEOs. Globally, women made up only 5% of the CEOs appointed in 2020. In the UK, women account for just 6% of FTSE 100 CEOs. This means that millions of women, both in the UK and the USA, are led and managed by men within the workplace. Men who potentially don't possess the understanding and skill set to lead and manage women efficiently, due to their lack of awareness of the natural biological processes of females. This can only be a bad thing for any organisation hence the urgency for more awareness.

8

Ageism, Menopause and Gender Identity

Menopause is another natural female process that needs more attention and awareness in the workplace. Menopause happens when a woman's oestrogen levels naturally decline. This happens usually around 45–55 years of age. Raising awareness of menopause within the workplace is crucial for organisations in the new normal. According to the Chartered Institute of Personnel and Development (CIPD), women over the age of fifty are the fastest-growing segment of the workforce, with six out of ten women saying menopause has a negative impact on their work. When we look at the great resignation and the fact that mid-level employees aged 25–45 years old are quitting at the highest rate. If menopause isn't addressed and managed in the workplace, employers could see more females of menopausal age quitting in the new normal, creating a further burden for employers.

With this demographic being the fastest growing and, more than likely, the most experienced and valued, it could spell disaster for female-dominated sectors such as health and social care. In these sectors, women represent 78% of the workforce. In education, women represent 70% of the workforce. A lack of experienced employees in these sectors will have multiple socioeconomic consequences. They'll have an immediate impact on the quality of life for the people directly benefiting from the work by these sectors. We're talking specifically about children, young adults, the education system, the sick, the confined, the disabled, the debilitated, and those from impoverished communities. The most vulnerable parts of our society that deserves the most protection and support. A part of society that a healthy, robust person, can become a part of, in a blink of an eye via an accident or a physical or mental health issue.

During menopause, women can experience cramps, heavy bleeding, and hot flushes like the menstrual cycle, affecting their work performance, productivity, and attendance. The major difference being the menstrual cycle lasts 2–7 days, whilst menopause can last for around seven years, with some women experiencing it for up to fourteen years. During menopause, women will experience night sweats and the inability to sleep, weight gain, depression, and anxiety, along with mood swings, fatigue, issues with bladder control and urinary tract infections. The severity of the symptoms can differ according to the individual's genetics and by race and ethnicity. An aspect of menopause employers and managers need to be mindful of that relates to the race issue.

There are stages to menopause. Perimenopause is the transitional period before menopause, and can start in women as early as their 30s. An age group that falls directly into the mid-level employee demographic of the great resignation with the highest resignation rates. Perimenopause means "around menopause" and refers to the time when a woman's body naturally transitions to menopause. Perimenopause, on average, lasts about four years. However, for some women, it can last a decade.

During Perimenopause, women can experience irregular periods, urinary tract infections, breast tenderness, premenstrual syndrome (PMS), headaches, and heart palpitations similar to having anxiety or a panic attack. Work-life will be affected because of the associated symptoms, such as forgetfulness and difficulty concentrating. The loss of sex drive and fertility issues can affect relationships. With mental health, it can bring about the onset of depression, anxiety, and panic attacks. A combination of these factors can also lead to alcohol and substance misuse, social isolation, and suicidal ideation.

There's the self-consciousness of getting older for a woman also associated with menopause. Ageing is a process that some women struggle to deal with because of societal pressures placed on women. The beauty and fashion industry pushes the myth of eternal beauty and youth on women from a young age and stays consistent with that message throughout their lives. This ideology of being ever youthful can lead to being embarrassed about getting older and can stifle conversations around menopause by women, thus contributing to the stigma surrounding the topic.

I remember as a child being told off by my mum for asking a woman her age. I was told, "you never ask a lady her age." I was never given a logical explanation for it, leaving me confused as a kid. I was told "you just don't," because "it's good manners." This was in the late 80s and since that day I know better, but as a grown-up, I don't believe it's healthy for the society we now live in. Women start the menstrual cycle as young as eight years old and most by around the age of twelve. As an adult, women go from pregnancy to motherhood to menopause. Should age, therefore, not be a badge of honour for a woman? I'm unsure about the consensus on what women of today feel about being open about age, or a man asking them their age, but I'd like to put my thoughts out there. I'm not fully convinced that this form of "good manners" is healthy for a society that seeks gender appreciation and workplace parity.

A study conducted by Dermstore, a U.S.-based skincare and beauty company, found that 28% of women under twenty-five regularly worry about signs of ageing. It's shocking that women so young are thinking along those lines. This worry of ageing increased to 42% for those aged 25–34, again, just way too young to worry about ageing. This age bracket can be considered the prime of life and the peak of one's powers for both men and women. There's a further increase in the worry of ageing, with 54% for women aged 35–44 years old. The study, however, found this worry decreases after the age of 55. That's still five decades of worrying about the inevitable and possibly speeding up the process. This indicates many people only consider themselves young for the first 25 years of an eight-decade lifespan. This is a farcical and unhealthy perception of age relative to the lifespan, the world seems to currently hold.

Ageism for men and women needs to be debunked. As a forty-four-year-old, I can confidently say that in the first forty years of our lives, we are young. There was nothing I could do physically at twenty years old, I could not do at forty years old. At forty I was also a much more rounded person.

I was the fittest I had ever been between the age of 35–40 years old. This was when I was training at the same intensity at a professional boxing level with my cousin Wadi Camacho, who was the UK Commonwealth cruiserweight boxing champion at the time.

Posing at the Olympic training camp in Walzc, Poland in 2016

Learning from the pros with Otto Wallin, Wadi Camacho and WBO World Champion Krzysztof Głowacki

Looking a bit short around pro cruiserweights and heavyweights at the Krzysztof Głowacki's training camp in Poland

In my office in Shoreditch with Wadi Camacho and my daughter
posing with the Commonwealth Cruiserweight belt in 2018

**Me in the ring at the Troxy in 2017, aged 39.
Fighting a 22-year-old amateur boxer!**

Now I'm not comparing my physical condition at this age to a woman and their biological journey. There's no comparison, men have it a lot easier. Nevertheless, what I was capable of between the age of 35–40 years old and what women such as Connie Dennison who taught Yoga into her 90s, Harriet Thompson who completed the Rock'n'roll San Diego Marathon aged 91, Ernestine Sheperd the oldest female bodybuilder aged 75, Donna Vano the oldest professional competing snowboarder at 61, and Eileen Olszewski who switched from ballet to boxing aged 46 and became the oldest world champion in the entire sport of boxing. All of which is proof, as humans from birth to at least forty, are young, and mentally and physically capable of anything. Please let no one convince you otherwise.

I attended Ironman in both Finland and Switzerland with my good friend Graham Shapiro, who was raising money for his charity, The Graham Shapiro Foundation. This charity supports mental health, well-being, innovation, and young entrepreneurialism in the UK. Graham took part in the gruelling competition in his late 40s. There were men and women well into their 60s competing. Most female competitors were of perimenopausal and menopausal age. The oldest person ever to complete Ironman was in Kona, Hawaii, in 2018, which was eighty-five-year-old Hiromu Inada. When you consider such feats by human beings, it's no wonder Socrates said, "It is a shame for a man to grow old without seeing the beauty and strength of which his body is capable." The same goes for women!

The Ironman event isn't for the light-hearted. It comprises a lake swim of 3.8km, a run of 26.2 miles, and a cycle of 112 miles non-stop. Most people in their 20s couldn't complete Ironman even with solid training. Therefore, when we hit seventy years old, that might be a good time to consider ourselves old and grow old gracefully, or disgracefully. Who cares? Even then, Hiromu Inada would possibly disagree. For a man like him, old is more than likely to be when a person is dead!

**Graham Completing Ironman Switzerland
in 2017 in 7hrs 23 minutes**

Finish line Selfie! Who says being in your 40's is old?

So, let's get some real perspective on age, as we're victims of our own self-manipulative ageist tactics, viewpoints, and perceptions that are mind-bogglingly brainless. The time has come to stop defining age with a number, or by what the beauty, fashion industry, or society and social media may define. The time has come to stop defining age according to how your face looks in a mirror. We should define age by how we feel, our determination, and what we're capable of. That is the only true measurement of age. When we look at age this way, we'll discover that some twenty-five-year-olds are older than some forty-five-year-olds. Employers with ageist management and recruitment processes should be mindful of what they're potentially missing out on.

Age is a number, and an irrelevant one. Employers in the new normal should be mindful of that fact. A forty-five-year-old may be a much better fit for the job, than the prettier or younger twenty-five-year-old. I have lived experience of this as a CEO when I was recruiting for a bookkeeper. In my mind, I thought

I should take on a young person with a sharp mind for the fast-paced role, to keep up with the hundreds of invoices we dealt with monthly. After interviewing multiple candidates, the person I found for the role was a lady in her 70s who possessed one of the most solid and sharpest numerical minds I've ever come across in my professional career.

With recruitment, employers need to focus on the person as much as the CV and gauge them human to human. As an employer, if you're trashing CVs because of a name, a person's age, or gender, recognise that there's no underpinning rationale for this recruitment process. That type of thinking is nothing but bad decision-making and leadership. This toxic preconceived notion of age in society, and the workplace, can be the reason that some women fear bringing up menopause with their employers. In fear that they may not get a promotion, a new job, or be viewed as difficult to manage if menopause is mentioned. Gendered ageism is a growing concern for women. According to Catalyst, a global organisation with a focus on intersectionality and consults organisations on how to build better workplaces for women, they found that older women were marginalised by what they called "lookism." This is where being youthful and attractive had major benefits, putting women under a microscope as they aged.

The study found that younger women under the age of forty-five had double the rate of callbacks for a second interview compared to older women. This is a regressive recruitment path for organisations as women over fifty-five are the fastest growing and most skilled demographic. They will account for more than a third of the U.S. workforce from 2016 to 2026. Between 2007 and 2013, the unemployment rate for older women over sixty-five skyrocketed from 14% to 50% in the USA. The study also found that older women had a higher rejection rate than older men for jobs, and 61% of workers in the USA over forty-five reported witnessing or experiencing ageism in the workplace. This was backed up by research by Forbes in collaboration with Out-Wit Inc, a women-owned marketing consulting company that studied responses from 729 women from the U.S., Canada, the UK, and Europe. The study found that 80% experienced gendered ageism, 33% felt they couldn't get a job or interview because of their age, and 47% reported that younger colleagues got more attention.

Ageism not only affects women. Insurance giant Hiscox conducted a study in 2019 called Ageism in the Workplace. They found that less than one-third of women felt age was a barrier to new employment at forty-years-old compared to 3% of men. This may be a sign that age discrimination could be decreasing for women in the UK due to awareness already raised. The study also found that 50% of workers witnessed age discrimination, 62% didn't speak out due to fear of retaliation by their employer, and 43% left their jobs after experiencing or witnessing age discrimination. These findings should raise eyebrows and ring some alarm bells for those working in HR.

It's essential in the new normal that employers are aware that ageism affects both men and women. However, menopause isn't something men must deal with alongside age discrimination, which must be considered for better management of women. Employers need to remember that at this stage in a woman's life, they deal with many other complexities outside of the work environment while experiencing perimenopause and menopause. Women at this age may care for children, grandchildren, ageing parents, or even their spouses. A lot of women also deal with the drama of raising adolescent teenagers, on top of juggling work and family demands whilst experiencing daily symptoms of menopause. Employers must be mindful of this extra and heavy burden on women in the workplace.

The menopausal stage of a woman's life is a pressure cooker for mental health risk factors. Menopause is connected to the exacerbation and onset of chronic physical health issues such as thyroid issues, high blood pressure and cholesterol, arthritis, asthma, and kidney issues. Menopause is the perfect example of why, in the new normal, employees must be managed like family or friends, incorporating a person's personal and professional life. There's no better way to manage people in the new normal. As a man and a CEO that lead a team of fifty women over ten years, when I researched menopause for this chapter, I was shocked at the impact it has on women and embarrassed at my lack of knowledge and understanding on the matter. Honestly, it made me glad I was a man, knowing I'd never have to go through such major biological changes to my body and mind.

You only have to look at organisations like Red Hot Mamas, an organisation that provides menopause education and support programs in the United States and Canada. The founder, Karen Giblin, created the organisation and concept because of her disruptive menopausal symptoms that happened after surgery for a total abdominal hysterectomy and bilateral oophorectomy. Those aren't considerations a man will ever need to have in his life because of a natural biological process. As a man, getting older means everything gets more gruelling and harder to recover from. I couldn't imagine having to deal with something like menopause, alongside what ageing naturally throws at you. Therefore, being mentally well and having a supportive employer and community at this stage of a woman's life are essential.

The problem is that most men, male CEOs, and managers don't have that awareness, leaving a gaping void in effectively managing female employees. Combined with the fact that men hold a much higher prevalence in management roles, this lack of awareness becomes a two-fold blow to effectively managing women in the workplace. Even men who have partners going through menopause lack awareness of the true impact of it. For a lot of men, it's simply something women go through, and like the menstrual cycle, it's best left to women to deal with. That can, and does, lead to many relationship issues. Men are wired to protect and provide. Therefore, if men were more educated on these topics, millions of men around the world could be more involved and more supportive of menopause both at home and within the workplace.

Due to this lack of education and awareness by male managers on menopause, there will be a disconnect in the workplace when men manage women. A report compiled by Manchester Metropolitan University in association with Talking Menopause, an organisation that works to affect a culture change in organisations around menopause, found that 91% of respondents suggested there was little to zero acknowledgement regarding menopause at work. Women also suggested they had to hide their menopausal symptoms. The report also found that 70% of women in menopause suggested they had moderate to zero confidence in discussing menopause at work.

It seems ridiculous that in a country such as the UK, we're so far behind on such matters. It's utterly unfair to the female workforce, which makes up almost half of the UK workforce. Bloomberg reported in 2021 that over 900,000 women quit UK jobs because of menopause. They reported that menopause productivity losses globally topped $150 billion a year. This should ring alarm bells for employers worldwide. Over the pond, in the USA, women make up almost 60% of the workforce. There are over 60 million women over the age of fifty in America. One billion women worldwide will experience menopause by 2025, menopause training and education are a must for managing women in the new normal on a global level.

I've spotlighted the implications regarding the disconnect between men and menopause, but this lack of awareness also extends to women. Bonafide, a company that sells products to treat women's health conditions, conducted the State of Menopause Study. A study of 1,039 women with ages ranging from forty to sixty-five across the United States. It found that one-third (29%) of women in the USA never sought information about menopause before they experienced it. This is homogeneous to the reactive approach many people have to mental ill health because of the taboo and stigma associated with those conversations. We are all aware of the devastating consequences of this non-proactive approach to mental health. Worryingly, because of the stigma associated with menopause, conversations and awareness of menopause seems to have followed suit.

Bonafide found that almost half of women (45%) didn't know the difference between perimenopause and menopause. One-fifth (20%) of women surveyed had experienced menopausal symptoms for a year or more before seeking professional health care, and 34% weren't formally assessed or diagnosed as menopausal. Also, 73% reported they weren't currently treating their menopausal symptoms, which included hot flashes (16%), weight gain (15%), difficulties with sleep (14%), and night sweats (14%). They were just getting on with it, as so many do with poor mental health symptoms. The survey also uncovered generational differences with 84% of women saying they aren't using the same treatment as their mothers and only 9% discussing menopause with their mothers. This is shocking, and it's important to ask why this is happening. This lack of awareness regarding menopause by women leaves women unprepared for what menopause will inevitably bring, thus increasing risk factors for mental ill health.

In the UK, a survey conducted by Ipsos MORI for the British Menopause Society found that 1 in 2 women aged 45-65, go through menopause with no professional medical consultation. About 50% of women in this survey claimed menopause negatively affected their home and sex life. In the workplace, 90% of women said their workplace offered no help or support regarding menopause. In the workplaces that recognise the existence of menopause, only 5% offer free advice, only 3% have policies regarding menopause and only 3% of line managers are given relevant training. How shocking when you consider women represent 51% of the UK population, around 28.5 million people!

The UK is leading the charge globally for developing practices and policies that will establish a more menopausal-friendly culture within workplaces. I hope this book and this chapter play a small part in this movement, helping to raise awareness amongst managers and employers about this essential topic. In February 2022, the UK established the UK Menopause Taskforce. The task force seeks to tackle the issues around menopause in the workplace. This includes tackling taboos and stigma associated with menopause and increasing access to treatment which will benefit millions of women in the UK. This doesn't mean, however, that employers and managers should get complacent and leave it to the government to lead the way on this matter. Organisations did that with mental health and that didn't turn out well.

Employers and managers can learn a lot about what not to do with menopause, simply by looking at how organisations have dealt with mental health since the introduction of the Health and Safety at Work Act in 1974. This act is the primary piece of legislation covering occupational health and safety in Great Britain and led to First Aid at Work becoming a legal duty for employers in the UK. This happened via the Health and Safety (First-Aid) Regulations Act in 1981. Over the next forty-odd years, our workplaces became some of the safest in the world outside of the construction sector, with physical safety. Employers, however, overlooked the importance of the "mental health" part under Section 2 of the Health and Safety at Work Act. Where its states that employers have a general duty of care to ensure the health, safety, and welfare of all their employees, including employees' mental health. Unlike First Aid at Work which became a legal obligation for employers, mental health remained a recommendation, and the consequences are staggering!

As a nation, we must ask ourselves if MHFA became a legal duty in 1981, like First Aid at Work. Would employers be losing £53-56 Billion because of poor mental health every year? An increase of 25% since the start of the pandemic, and equivalent to an eye-watering 2.6% of annual GDP, according to Deloitte's Mental Health and Employers report released in March 2022. Are those who work in risk management picking up on this data, or even aware of it? All employers in the new normal should sign the Where's Your Head At manifesto, and all employees should sign the petition. Natasha Devon MBE, a mental health campaigner, is leading this campaign alongside MHFAE to make MHFA a legal requirement in the workplace. Getting this law passed could be a revolution for the mental health of the UK.

Menopause and the gender issue mustn't be dealt with in the same dilettante manner as mental health by employers and managers in the new normal. Mental health is a hot topic now, especially since the pandemic. That, however, doesn't mean mental health is sorted. In fact, far from it. Talking about a topic is healthy, but inaction is unhealthy. Employers need to be mindful that talking about something doesn't equate to action or even progress. The only thing mental health being a hot topic has done, is uncovered just how much more work there still needs to be done. It's no different from menopause. Action is vital in managing the female workforce in the new normal. Employers must be proactive and ensure managers, both male and female, are trained, literate, and pushing the agenda on the menopause issue.

Like mental health at work, menopause awareness and literacy aren't a tick-box exercise, it's one that will be a constant work in progress for all organisations in the new normal. The same level of priority and process employers take to eradicate the stigma around mental health, should be on par with eradicating the stigma and taboo around menopause. The best practice for organisations is to implement a robust and supportive framework for menopause awareness and literacy. This can be done via menopause coaching and consultancy. As I mentioned in "The Race Issue" chapter, it's essential to use PGM to consult and coach on race issues. With menopause, it's best practice for organisations to use women with lived experiences of menopause to coach and consult.

Davina McCall, shed some light on menopause and how it affects a woman's mind and body, and its impact on women in the workplace, in Channel 4's *Davina McCall: Sex, Myths, and the Menopause*. This documentary is a great starting point for business leaders and managers to acquire some understanding of menopause and its impact on the workplace. The first-time menopause had my attention was through LinkedIn and the work of Amantha King at Amantha King Coaching. Amantha is consistent with the message on menopause and is passionate about raising awareness of the topic through posts and multimedia. Following her work has been insightful and informative and has helped me in becoming more literate on menopause as a man, and an employer. Amantha represents the passionate individuals available, whom organisations should seek to forge alliances with in regard to menopause awareness and coaching

Gender Identity

Gender identity and literacy is a fresh new topic for most managers over a certain age, especially for those over the age of thirty. Traditionally, when we discuss gender, it was based on men and women, male or female. In the new normal, addressing gender identity in the workplace with the understanding and professionalism it requires is an essential skill for managers to possess. No matter where you stand on gender identity, it's impossible to create an inclusive workplace without inclusivity for all genders, and an understanding of trans and non-binary employee rights, needs, and wants. It can become overwhelming for both employers and managers, hence getting to grips with this topic is a must.

As I pointed out at the beginning of this chapter, the meaning of gender according to the Oxford English Dictionary is:

Either of the two sexes (male and female), especially when considered with reference to social and cultural differences rather than biological ones. The term is also used more broadly to denote a range of identities that do not correspond to established ideas of male and female. "A condition that affects people of both genders."

This part of the chapter is about becoming workplace literate on the second part of the definition of gender, where it says, "The term is also used more broadly to denote a range of identities that do not correspond to established ideas of male and female. 'A condition that affects people of both genders.'"

The first thing to acknowledge as an employer or manager is that "gender" is an identity, it's someone's sense of who they are. It's not the same as "sex" which relates to biological and physiological characteristics, such as genitals and chromosomes. Gender identity is about how a person identifies themselves regarding their gender, regardless of biological or physical characteristics. This means a person may identify themselves as male, female, both, and neither. They may also identify in some other category, despite their biological and physiological characteristics. This can sound or come across as confusing to some people, which is understandable but can be overcome through literacy on the subject.

It's wise to remember that we all have a unique window into the world. As employers and managers, it's important to recognise that gender identity is a tool to help a person feel comfortable in their skin, regardless of the gender they were born with. As with the right for a person to identify according to a gender of their choosing, another person has the same right not to identify a person in this way. That is an ongoing societal issue and debate, however, in the workplace, it's important to make space for it.

According to the Harvard Business Review, 12% of millennials in America identify as transgender or gender non-conforming, and most millennials believe gender is a spectrum rather than binary to man or woman. With Gen Z in America, 56% know a person using gender-neutral pronouns and 25% expect to be fluid with their gender during their lifetime. Research by VICE Magazine found that 41% of Gen Zs from western countries identify somewhere in between the masculine to feminine scale, hence the importance of being literate as employers and managers.

There are currently 72 genders and over 78 pronouns. There may be even more by the time I publish this book as the landscape on gender fluidity is constantly evolving, especially amongst Gen Zs who are every organisation's upcoming workforce. Pronouns are linguistic tools and terminology used to refer to people, for example, she/her/hers, he/him/his, that we use daily. In the

LGBTQIA+ communities, pronouns play an important part in the use of language. Pronouns are how people in the community acknowledge and identify themselves and how they'd like others to address and identify them.

With managing people, employers and managers must acknowledge that how a person identifies deserves to be accepted and respected. Managers must recognise that assuming someone's gender can be hurtful, just as illiterate language around race or sex can be hurtful. Being literate on gender and language as an employer or manager has a profound impact on mental health at work. A study conducted by the University of Texas found the risk of suicide and depression drops in transgender youth when allowed to use their chosen name and pronouns in places such as work, school, and home. Earlier studies showed that one out of three transgender youths reported considering suicide. In the UK, according to the Adult Psychiatry Morbidity Survey, 48% of trans people under twenty-six had attempted suicide, and 59% said they had at least considered doing so. This data is traumatic, and employers must do all they can to positively impact this data in the new normal via gender-literate management teams.

For better management of LGBTQIA+ employees, employers and managers must be literate on mental health within this community. LGBTQIA+ people are three times more likely to develop mental health issues and four times more likely to experience depression than the general population in the UK. According to NatCen Social Research, Britain's leading independent social research institute, which published "The experiences of UK LGBT+ communities during the COVID-19 pandemic" in November 2021. Found that self-harm, suicidal ideation, and suicide attempts increased, with younger LGBTQIA+ with trans people being the most affected. Experiences of harassment and violence outside the home increased along with online harassment during the pandemic. A study by Stonewall found that 50% of LGBTQIA+ people experienced depression and three in five experienced anxiety. One in eight LGBTQIA+ people aged 18–24 attempted suicide, and 50% of trans people thought about taking their own life.

As you can see, it's important for employers and managers to educate themselves on acceptable and respectful terminology. Working closely with current gender-fluid and trans employees for clarification is the best practice. This management strategy will go a long way in helping reduce the mental burden and prejudice that many in these communities experience daily. A person from the LGBTQIA+ community won't be upset the first time an employer or manager unintentionally gets language wrong, so don't be afraid to ask if in doubt. Most people from the LGBTQIA+ communities will be pleased to advise and help an employer avoid any assumptions and establish appropriate language and terminology. This will also make employees from these communities feel seen and heard within the organisation. This is the best type of allyship an employer can develop with employees from this community in the new normal. Organisational and managerial understanding of gender identity, terminology, and pronouns is an exemplary way to signal courtesy, respect, and acceptance. This type of hierarchical acknowledgement is a superlative affirmation of that allyship.

Employers should also remember that this approach to managing people from LGBTQIA+ communities will go a long way to keeping in line with the legal obligations that govern employers. The Equality Act 2010 says an employer cannot discriminate against a person because they're transsexual and when a person's gender identity differs from the sex assigned at birth. The Equality Act 2010: states "A person has the protected characteristic of gender reassignment if the person is proposing to undergo, is undergoing or has undergone a process (or part of a process) for the purpose of reassigning the person's sex by changing physiological or other attributes of sex."

In the new normal, managerial illiteracy on these matters should be considered discriminatory. Now, having said all of that, it doesn't mean every employer or manager needs to learn 72 new forms of management or 78 new pronouns to be effective in the new normal. Most employers and managers won't have all 72 genders or use all 78 pronouns for managing their team or department. The priority should always be on managing the genders and properly applying pronouns and terminology to employees incumbent in any team. A manager must grasp that, no matter what a person identifies as, they're human, with the same needs and wants as everyone else. On a management level, this simplifies something that may seem overwhelming to get to grips with, especially for older managers.

Therefore, in being literate and aware of the gender identity topic, employers and managers need to realise that it's more about understanding, using correct language, continuous learning, and the all-important human touch. The very basics of people management. When you look at it this way, the learning isn't as profuse as it may initially seem. Gender identity is something organisations in the new normal can work towards, alongside those incumbent employees that identify as gender fluid. This is best practice. Never underestimate the power of giving employees a platform to make a difference. As I've said before, an employer's most effective consultants will always be their existing employees.

9

Advancement in Technology and The Metaverse

I wrote this chapter during Mental Health Awareness Week 2022. The Mental Health Foundation had chosen loneliness as the theme for Mental Health Awareness Week. We've looked at loneliness and how technology affects mental health, organisations, and society because of the transition into hybrid working in the new normal. So, as I write this chapter, it feels like a sign I'm going in the right direction with this book.

When the world went into lockdown for the first time in 2020, March 2020 for the UK. None of us could've imagined the new working world that would emerge post-pandemic. Many of us had never heard of Teams or Zoom, let alone used the platforms or even uttered the words, "hybrid working," or "the new normal." As I've outlined in this book, especially with mental health and people management, the new normal is a massive opportunity to make things better for people and businesses. The positives for both people and businesses are abundant in the hands of adept and forward-thinking leaders and managers.

When it comes to technology, there are a few pitfalls that can be considered treacherous for employers and hazardous for mental health and society. Consider addiction to social media and screens, a relatively new obsession that society developed during the last decade. I was sixteen years old when I went to college in 1994. I was one of the few people at college with a mobile phone. In the following two years, every single person I knew had a mobile phone. Those days it was just calls and text messages, text messages being the cutting edge of mobile phone technology. Almost three decades later, we're all carrying smartphones which are so embedded in our lives some of us have become cyborg slaves to them. We stare at our smartphones so much; they may as well be biologically attached to our hands. I'm convinced if I streaked through a carriage on the London Underground, not one person would notice, everyone's too busy doom scrolling on their phones. It's a scary time, and I'm not just talking about the thought of me streaking through the London Underground!

We're at a time in civilisation where our phones only need to make a beep and we come running. No different to how a dog runs to its owner when it hears its owner's whistle. There are over 3.8 billion smartphone users in the world, and according to Virgin Mobile, smartphone users receive 427% more messages and notifications than they did a decade ago, users send 278% more messages. Phone addiction is real and linked to the term "nomophobia," or the fear of being without your smartphone. It affects our behaviour and is responsible for sleep deprivation, stress, loneliness, insecurity, and it aggravates anxiety, depression, and ADHD. It harms concentration, negatively affects grades and creates relationship issues. All this from one piece of tech that's become an addiction to be stared at constantly, like we're hypnotised. I aggressively try to cut down my phone use and check my screen time to reduce it week by week. Frustratingly, I still seem to use it for 2–3 hours a day, which is 14–21 hours a week. That is almost a day every week, staring at my phone. Do you know your screen time for your phone use?

When we combine all the other screens we stare at daily, such as televisions and computers, according to SWNS a UK and U.S.-based news and media company. The average American will spend forty-four years of their life staring at screens. In the UK, it's thirty-four years. Maybe you want to stop reading for a moment, take a deep breath, and let those statistics buffer. Gaming addictions, according to research by Game Quitters who are the largest support community for video game addiction. Around 3–4% of gamers are addicted, that's over 60 million people with video game addiction, and 90–99% of kids in the USA play video games along with 48% - 56% of young adults. The average age of a gamer is thirty-five years old, and the average age of a gaming addict is twenty-four years old. The global average for a binge gaming session is 5.1 hours.

In the new normal, we live our lives moving from one screen to another. We wake up with our phones, work on our laptops, move on to our televisions, and go to bed with our tablets or phone. For those who have read George Orwell's *1984,* where society is continuously monitored by screens and mass surveillance combined with people's blind acceptance of these facts, and no thought is given to privacy, mental health, or societal consequences. The book could easily have been named *2022.* What we must realise first as humans, then as employers and managers, is that this "living on a screen life" is the opposite of our human nature. When we go against our human nature, there are consequences. Those consequences are clear, abundant, visible, and costly, especially here in the West.

We are at a crossroads with technology. Technology is developing at a furious pace but seems to head in the opposite direction of our human needs. It's down to the leaders in big tech to instil some humanity in their technology this side of the pandemic. This is where future reputation, respectably, and the ability to attract the best future minds firmly lie for big tech. We've seen the damage unbridled uptake of technology can do to our lives over the last couple of decades. In the new normal, the development of future technology must be immersed in an awareness of human wellbeing. Organisations need to be mindful of taking on technology that only seeks to make the operation function better, with disregard for the human cost. If new technology implemented in the workplace doesn't consider the mental impact of its use, it should be considered unfit for purpose in the new normal.

We've seen the likes of Zoom and Teams become an integral part of work almost overnight, adding to daily screen time that already puts a person at a higher risk of poor mental and physical health. There will undoubtedly be further development of new technology to enhance or rival platforms such as Zoom or Teams, for work in the hybrid world. This new tech will more than likely immerse us even further into that high-risk digital world. Organisations will need to take full advantage of this new digital opportunity as we accelerate into the digital working world, but do so safely, with the human in mind. This book has highlighted the positives of hybrid working and how, if it's well managed, can be a godsend for both employer and employee.

In the new normal, due to advancements in technology, it's likely some organisations will go even further than the hybrid working contract, to attract and retain the best talent and to meet employee needs and wants. Organisations could counterbalance the impact of future screen immersion via full-time flexible working. Full-time flexible working is where an employee is contracted to, let's say, 37.5 hours a week, but can work whenever they feel, as long as the contracted hours are covered, and the tasks delegated are completed in time. Even though this won't decrease screen time, it will give an employee much more freedom and life compared to office-based, or hybrid working, which is still rigid in its working hours. With office and hybrid working, core hours worked still fall under the traditional 9 a.m. – 5 p.m. working day.

Not all organisations, and certain departments within organisations, will have the luxury of offering full-time flexible work. For example, construction, hospitality, blue light, and other frontline services may never have the luxury of full-time flexible work due to how the sector functions. However, for sectors, organisations, and departments that can, they'll be the future breadwinners for attracting and keeping the best talent. In the future, it's possible employees will have an option of two types of employer, the employer that offers hybrid working and the employer that offers flexible working. Take a wild guess where most employees will choose to be employed!

This could pose a major recruitment crisis for sectors and organisations that cannot function on full-time flexible work contracts. It may lead to fewer graduates and a lack of interest in jobs by workers for those sectors, leading to major issues in recruitment and retention. We're already seeing a glimpse of what can be, via the great resignation, when employees aren't happy. This will have far-reaching consequences for society since most sectors that can't offer full-time flexible work are sectors such as primary and secondary education, healthcare, emergency, and social services. All of which are vital to a healthy human population. Therefore, employers in sectors that cannot offer full-time flexible work must do everything they can to prepare and counterbalance this risk by implementing healthy people management practices, such as those described in this book. Managing people in the new normal via principles based on mental health and wellbeing, will go a long way to attracting and keeping employees, if full-time flexible work becomes a reality in the future due to technological advancements.

One of the best ways to counterbalance this "moth to a flame" type of attraction that full-time flexible working will have on workers, is by leveraging the human connection we have with each other. Employers in sectors that can't offer such flexibility, must get to work immediately, to create the perfect setting for our human nature, where being at work is more of a holistic and family-style experience. So, when employees see full-time flexible work becoming more common and consider it a potential option, they'll find it tempting but place the human connection at a higher or similar value. This brings us back to managing people with true regard for their human needs, it's the only way to nurture the human value connection.

Then there is the Metaverse. When I first watched Mark Zuckerberg's one-hour and seventeen-minute video, *The Metaverse and How We'll Build It Together*, I felt excited as I felt nauseous. The possibilities of the metaverse are limitless for organisations and the world. We, however, live in a world where people are already struggling with the impact of technology as it is, and their inability to live without staring at a screen. A fully immersive digital experience, such as the metaverse, can only add fuel to this fire if not appropriately managed and regulated.

The online environment has already created a subset of the human population that's addicted or dependent digitally. Many people struggle in managing their digital time in a healthy manner, in line with their natural human needs. Even as things are now digitally, we can still see, hear, and smell the real world around us. We still, for the most part, must use a screen to be connected digitally. All it takes is for the doorbell to ring, a bird to sing, your cat to jump on your lap, or your partner to call your name. We can immediately look away from our screens and engage with the real world, with real things, and real people.

Now to clarify, I'm not saying all technology in the new normal is bad for us. Technology is a much-needed tool for humanity to move forward in anything we wish to do. It's part of our civilisation, it has many benefits, and it is here to stay. The metaverse is exciting, but it will be addictive for many. Being mindful of advancing technology, and its impact on our human essence, and nature, is key to healthy and happy humans. Companies developing, and organisations implementing such technology, both on a societal and organisational level, need to be mindful of the risks. The metaverse is the current digital world on steroids, one that carries major risk factors attached to mental health and wellbeing, impacting how organisations will need to manage people in the future.

The metaverse is a virtual-reality (VR) space where we can all interact with each other through avatars in a computer-generated environment. You can create your digital twin in the metaverse and go about your everyday business using the same headsets and glasses as used in virtual and augmented reality (AR) video games. The metaverse is a total immersion into the digital world and, for many, it will be a total disconnect between reality and the real physical world. Technology has been addictive, hence the need to be careful about what may happen if the metaverse becomes the next big thing in tech.

Imagine having a team meeting on a beach in Sri Lanka with all your colleagues. Imagine having an appraisal while driving Route 66 in a convertible mustang or your lunch break from a spaceship with a view of planet earth. Imagine teleporting from office to office to see colleagues you may never have met in other parts of the world, and then working on a project together in their office space. You can use the metaverse for work and then you and your colleagues can go to a digital bar or concert afterwards. It's the real world in a digital format that allows you to do so much more than you could ever dream of in the real world.

In the metaverse, if you're unhappy with your body you can change it, if you're unhappy with the way you look, you can change it, if you're unhappy with your wardrobe, you can change it, if you're unhappy with your social circle, you can meet new digital people from around the world without ever sitting on a plane. Your avatar doesn't even have to take a human form. You can be a robot or a fluffy bunny. You can have different avatars for work and social use. You can teleport into different worlds. You can teleport back in time and see how the Romans lived, visit another planet, or see a T-Rex in the Jurassic. Now, just stop to think for a moment about how addictive it will be. The problem is that it's not reality, and the worry is how people will deal with the real world when they're much happier and content in the metaverse.

The metaverse is moving fast. Microsoft has created their own metaverse. It's fast becoming a functioning world with machine learning, blockchain technology, and digital currencies all playing their part. You can buy land and real estate in the metaverse. Commerce will be a big part of the metaverse. According to Forbes, companies such as PwC, JP Morgan, HSBC, and Samsung have invested in prime plots of land in the metaverse ready for development. Yes, you can buy and sell digital land, property, and much more. It makes me want to turn the electricity off and hug the nearest human.

The advancement of technology leaves many organisations in a precarious situation, where they're damned if they do, and damned if they don't. If the metaverse becomes widely used in society, like Facebook and Instagram, or if it becomes widely used in the workplace, like Teams and Zoom, which is more than likely to happen. This new digital world fast approaching will create further challenges in people management and wellbeing. Therefore, it's imperative organisations do all that can be done for better management of people, before technology such as the metaverse comes along, and throws a massive spanner in the works with mental health and wellbeing in the workplace.

There's a strong possibility the metaverse will be the next stage of the internet. It's as dangerous as it is exciting. The metaverse will create new economic opportunities whilst posing a risk to existing businesses if they don't get in front of it and explore the opportunity it provides. For example, on the most basic level, I run MHFA courses online using Zoom and I advertise these courses on Google via my website. In the metaverse, I can deliver these same courses online but within a virtual classroom setting overlooking a beach in Hawaii with people from all over the world. Now, as a business owner, if I find advertising for my courses on the metaverse to be more lucrative than Google, I will stop advertising on Google. Therefore, the metaverse is a threat to the advertising revenue of Google. This can lead to Google becoming an obsolete platform for businesses to advertise. I can also go to a virtual library in the metaverse and get any information I want, instead of "Googling" it. Then I realise I don't need Zoom anymore, as the metaverse setting offers my learners a superior learning experience, thus making Zoom defunct in my business operations. Then I realise I don't need my website as I can take potential customers to my online virtual gallery, and showcase my products and services. Therefore, the services of my web designer, pay-per-click (PPC), and search engine optimisation (SEO) marketing providers are no longer needed.

Online marketing companies will have no choice but to get involved with the metaverse and offer metaverse marketing services in the new normal. The metaverse could leave social media marketing, PPC marketing, and SEO marketing practices obsolete. As a reader, you should be able to gauge the power and possibilities of the metaverse, and be in no doubt regarding the impact it could have on the way we live and work. It's everything that is digitally possible rolled into virtual reality and will more than likely become a game changer like Google and Facebook were in the early 2000s.

The metaverse won't only immerse us in the digital world, but it will mix realities via VR or AR glasses. This means the digital world will merge into the physical world via these glasses. A person can put the glasses on and interact digitally with holograms and augmented realities in the physical world. Therefore, you don't have to be in your home with a headset on. You can be digitally connected via these glasses, constantly merging the digital and physical worlds. This will blur the two realities which may become problematic for some people. A person using these glasses in public will look no different to a person in psychosis, talking to themselves, behaving oddly, and seeing things the average person doesn't. This has the potential to create unique social issues and divisions in society.

My concern after watching Mark Zuckerberg's video is where he states Meta is about connecting people to people, whereas other tech companies, connect people to technology, and the thing that matters most is people. Therefore, it was disappointing that nothing in the video discussed online mental health and wellbeing, as the technology has the potential to educate billions of people around the world. Something that's been severely lacking in technology that came before. Even in the "building responsibly" part of the video, there are discussions about privacy, security, and inclusion, yet no mention of the potential psychological impact of its use and how the company will attenuate those risks. With mental health and wellbeing, the metaverse is uncharted territory. Therefore, it's surprising that, as an organisation with so many great minds, haven't put mental health as a centrepiece of the metaverse.

The metaverse will be a gift and a curse. It has the potential to be the cure or further participate in the cause of our current digital addiction and isolation. The direction the metaverse will head will all depend on the leadership at Meta and their understanding of mental health and its importance. The company should invest as heavily in mental health within the metaverse, as it's done with all other areas of development in order to protect users. Prompts, activities, notifications, and education in wellbeing to counterbalance any health risks from time spent in digital, or mixed realities could go a long way towards the health and safety of users. The importance of disconnecting and the dangers of overuse should be a core focus. Individual user reports and organisational reports sent to managers in organisations that use the metaverse, outlining guidelines on what an individual must do in the physical world to counterbalance the impact of time spent digitally, could lead to revolutionary change in the way we look after ourselves in our digital future.

Until then, it is down to individual users and organisations that will use the metaverse to govern themselves with digital health and safety. That, however, hasn't played out too well so far in the current digital world. The danger is if people and organisations don't take this approach, it will create a subset of humans that are disconnected and out of touch with the real world. This is already a reality for many in the current digital world via the use of screens. Total immersion and mixed realities have the potential to exacerbate this problem, creating a subset of humans that truly can't function in the real world.

For some, dealing with everyday life in the real world could become as problematic and difficult as withdrawal symptoms from an addictive drug. For organisations, it could create immense challenges to managing and engaging people in real-world scenarios. Therefore, organisations must take an urgent and proactive approach to people management challenges they already face with hybrid working and other challenges that the new normal has created. If organisations do not get ahead of this before the metaverse becomes a reality, there will more than likely be dire consequences.

There is an urgency here due to the speed at which technology is evolving. If a competitor gains the upper hand due to using the metaverse in their business operation, everyone in the market will follow. This is why organisations must rid themselves of their dinosaurs and get the right leaders in place now. If organisations don't have mental health and wellbeing right by the time the metaverse becomes as well used as Teams or Zoom, the challenges for better management and wellbeing of employees may actually become insurmountable. The metaverse and rapidly evolving technology are good reasons why organisations can't keep scratching their heads, sitting on their hands, and relying on dinosaurs in the new normal. This is the opportune moment, so act now!

10

Departmental Localisation

Over the course of this book, I've mentioned the importance of employers conversing with their staff frequently. I cannot over-emphasise the importance of such conversations for managing people in the new normal. Departmental Localisation (DL) is a simple, five-step strategy I developed over the years as a CEO to get to know my employees. It's been further developed over the last three years to incorporate the mental health aspect. DL is a strategy organisations will find useful in getting to know the needs and wants of their employees on an individual level, department by department.

DL is based on having meaningful and personal conversations with employees. I've found that talking to employees seems to be something that scares organisations, and many are unsure of how best to do it. Reluctancy to converse with employees may be due to employers not wanting to open the floodgates, and being exposed to what materialises. Some organisations would rather not open that can of worms. Other organisations may simply not care. Ignorance may be bliss temporarily but will eventually turn into a nightmare for employers in the new normal. It's already happening with the great resignation, strikes and protests in various sectors during the last few months of 2022 in the UK. It's a sign of things to come. Rishi Sunak the current Prime Minister, along with the several that came before in a matter of months, are still not making the connection between a healthy economy and a healthy workforce.

Talking to employees terminates the ridiculous top-down approach to well-being in people management. Some organisations like to implement the top-down approach because senior managers and CEOs feel they know best. This approach is usually taken to tick boxes and get a certificate on a wall, so CEOs feel like they've done their bit and line managers feel like they've completed a task. The incoming Gen Z workforce will perceive this as organisational laziness and lack of care for employees. As the great resignation has proven, that's the same for existing employees. Sticking to pre-pandemic management practices in the new normal is regressive and will become a stumbling block in meeting an employer's social, moral and corporate responsibilities.

The term DL may initially sound complicated, but I developed and built the strategy on a foundation of simplicity and simple common sense. You don't need an MBA to understand it or a rocket scientist to implement it. By design, it's easily applicable but needs to be done correctly for the best results. The strategy is based on the theory that there are no generic or off-the-shelf solutions to wellbeing in the workplace. DL determines that, to understand an organisation and the needs and wants of its workforce, management practices must be personalised, localised, unique, and specific to each department. Only then can generic solutions be applied if relevant. Think of each department in an organisation as its own organisation. That is DL.

Generic solutions for wellbeing in the workplace, along with the lack of MHFA training, is one reason EAPs fall short, and employees don't engage with such initiatives, leaving organisations and managers bemused. Generic solutions and the lack of MHFA training are contributing factors to why mental health at work has been a big issue long before the pandemic. Organisations and managers must remember that the 57% of days taken off in the UK due to mental health issues are a pre-pandemic statistic. The data on mental health in the workplace proves that something is broken with the implementation and engagement in mental health at work. This is why I created self-paced first aid for mental health courses that are accredited, as a crucial addition to EAP's for organisations.

DL is based on the theory that the needs and wants of an organisation, aren't generic, but specific to each department within an organisation. Take two departments in the same organisation. One department is filled with people in their 20s, the other is filled with people in their 40s. The needs and wants of those departments will undoubtedly be different due to multiple factors and variables. These factors and variables are local and specific to the culture, productivity, performance alongside personal and professional circumstances of the employees of each department.

Factors and variables can be things such as age, financial situation, family situation, housing situation, gender, mental and physical health, disabilities, resilience and adaptability, personality types and experience of the people within a specific department. DL is a flexible and fluid strategy that organisations can further develop to make it even more unique and specific to their departments. It gives the flexibility for organisations to ask questions and dig deeper based on a core set of factors. DL is a continuous work in progress regarding people management and its application.

What organisations will find by applying DL is that each department has its own unique set of needs and wants. Those needs and wants are the true focus of better people management. The lack of this true focus is why organisations aren't getting engagement with their off-the-shelf or generic solutions in their

EAPs, and why mental health in the workplace is at an all-time low. I used DL when I was the CEO of the London Makeup School and The London Hair Academy. At the academy, over 80% of the staff were freelance hairdressers and makeup artists. The freelance team also included bookkeepers, business consultants, web designers and marketers. Freelancers are their own small businesses specialising in their sector and are essential workers for organisations that require their services. Historically, they've always been difficult to manage and gel into an existing full-time workforce. Freelancers love the freedom of coming and going and working with multiple employers.

Employment laws in the UK don't allow for appraisal systems to be used for non-full-time staff, this can be stifling for company culture, especially for organisations highly dependent on the skill set of a freelance workforce. There's no law, however, saying you can't have unofficial one on ones with freelance staff and get to know their needs and wants. This is crucial for any organisation that depends on a freelance workforce. I implemented parts of DL into my appraisal systems with full-time staff and one on ones with my freelance team. The result was exponential growth, and the academy became the highest-rated and reviewed on Google in the world. The staff base continually grew and staff turnover for several years was almost non-existent.

That's a snippet of the potential of DL that organisations can leverage and benefit from in the new normal. Those results wouldn't have been possible if it wasn't for the collaboration between freelance and full-time staff. DL enabled the two groups and several departments to appreciate and work well together towards the organisation's vision. This was simply done via recognising each group's needs and wants on a departmental level and acting on those needs and wants. Thus, creating a culture where most employees felt involved, heard, and taken care of, or felt the organisation was trying to, regardless of their work status or job role.

One of the most insightful bits of data I found through DL was regarding employees and freelance staff that worked for both the hair and makeup teams. The two teams functioned, operated, and were managed differently by managers with their own unique management styles. The data from the DL process showed the needs and wants of employees changed depending on the team they worked for, even though it was the same person within the same organisation. The application of DL and the development of HR and people management practices that came into fruition resulted in our Investors in People standard elevating from Core to Gold in two years. It also led me to win one of the most coveted awards in HR and people management. The Investors in People Manager of the Year Award in 2018.

Once an organisation implements DL, it will discover that the finance department feels and sees things differently from the IT department. HR feels and sees things differently from the sales department, yet it's all within the same organisation. This is the reason I've described the top-down approach to well-being and people management as ridiculous. An effective EAP can only be built by talking to staff to find out what they really need, and the DL strategy is a great way to do it. DL can help in identifying appropriate EAPs for each department in an organisation. EAPs that are of true value to the employees of that department, and not some generic assistance available to anyone. The information gathered provides a platform where bottom-up and top-down needs and wants to come together, to find that all-important "happy place!" Identification of appropriate EAPs for each department can be cost-efficient for an organisation.

When EAPs and people management practices are informed and developed via a collaborative process, it becomes powerful and efficient, applicable to each department within an organisation. This approach ensures that every department has its own EAPs and people management practices that work for and are built by the individuals within that department. Implementing EAPs in any other fashion, as data proves, is defunct. It's like waving a magic wand and hoping everything will be OK. It shows a true lack of insight into human needs and nature, and illiteracy of mental health and well-being in the workplace.

DL can be initialised with two simple questions put forward to staff.

1. Write three things your employer can do to help you with your wellbeing at work (keep it personal to you, your job role, and your day-to-day).

2. Write three things you can do at work that can improve the wellbeing of others around you. (This can be as personal as speaking with a person who hasn't been themselves lately, all the way to changes in company policy regarding mental health and wellbeing)

These two simple questions will open a treasure trove of invaluable, unique, and department/person-specific data for organisations. Organisations pay large sums in consultancy fees to gather such data, yet managers can gather it for free and with a better understanding of the data via the DL strategy. I've applied DL through my first aid for mental courses, specifically my NUCO Supervising First Aid for Mental Health Level 3 course. I've done this with my clients, ranging from small independent chemists to large construction companies and huge multinationals in pharmaceuticals and shipping. The data gathered has been invaluable and invigorating for managers and employers.

One of my clients, a multi-national PLC, trained forty-eight staff from offices in the UK and Ireland. The DL process gathered 288 data points from the forty-eight staff. The data gathered was insightful for managers. Through the data, we discovered a lot of everyday stressors at work were physical. There was also a sense of relief from employees because of the safe space created by the DL process where a third party was in control (me as the instructor), rather than a manager. This was because employees felt some stressors, especially physical stressors, were too small to bring up with their managers but had a substantial negative impact on their day-to-day. Workplace physical stressors, such as a lack of chill-out and dining spaces, creaking chairs, dim lights, lack of plants, availability of water, and windows that don't open, came up. It also highlighted other stressors, such as frustrating software and managerial and operational processes that needed improvement including managers themselves.

DL highlighted and identified themes in the data where several members of staff would mention the same stressor. Themes in the data represent areas of priority and urgency for organisations to fix. Another interesting point in the data collected was that some issues were quick and easy fixes for an employer. Stressors such as dim lights and creaking chairs, lack of plants and availability of water. Acting on these quick fixes will have an immediate positive impact on staff morale. Staff will feel seen and heard, it will show employees that the data collected via the DL process wasn't another futile "do-gooder" exercise. Too many organisations are guilty of futile "do-gooder" exercises that amount to nothing. Information is gathered, goes up the chain, and nothing comes of it. Employees are bored stiff with such practices. DL is no different. If there's no action from the data, it means nothing. Action is king!

Quick fixes are tangible evidence an employer is listening but also acting, the power of which shouldn't be underestimated. Quick fixes give an employer breathing space when more time is needed to act on and implement areas that aren't quick fixes. Sometimes, employees' needs and wants can't be met by employers. Frequently, I've trained organisations that operate from buildings without windows that open to let fresh air in. The entire internal climate is controlled via the air conditioning system, the same as with many hotels. Due to the design of the building, opening windows will never be an option. If an organisation can meet as many other needs as possible that come to light via the DL process, it will be easier for employees to accept and appreciate the things that cannot be changed when communicated well. Employers can go as far as giving employees a timeline of action. Once again, simple practices like this will go a long way toward staff morale and a healthy culture in the workplace.

Now, I'm sure that many employers and managers reading this will think DL can be applied via staff surveys, team meetings, appraisals and one on ones. Yes, it can. It was done similarly in my previous role as a CEO, and it worked well. It was by accident I discovered how much better it works integrated into an MHFA course. It was only when I got into the MHFA field I realised the deep connection between the two. When I first became an MHFA instructor, courses were generally booked by organisations as opposed to individuals. I'd estimate that, for my organisation, over 80% of bookings come from organisations booking employees. As I taught the courses, I realised mental health at work was the most important topic for these organisations and one of the main reasons they booked the courses. The pandemic had escalated that importance.

As an expert in people management, I found the course content lacking in mental health in the workplace. This was no fault of the governing body, as the courses covered a range of relevant topics that needed to be covered to a certain level. There were also time constraints that needed to be considered. An MHFA course is two days long with a lot of important content. The courses were also developed pre-pandemic, so mental health at work learning wasn't as a hot topic as it was post-pandemic. The MHFAE courses don't allow you to add any content because of the way courses are licenced and the rules instructors are governed by. That, however, doesn't mean that organisations cannot apply DL themselves after taking MHFAE courses. The MHFAE course is, by a country mile, the best MHFA course on the market. A newly updated course was launched in the summer of 2022. It comes with an MHFA support app to help individuals and organisations leverage MHFA training and implement it in their lives and workplaces.

The NUCO course content allows for more flexibility. I integrated the initial DL process and the creation of a wellbeing menu with no impact on the existing content, which dramatically enhanced the existing content on mental health at work. The results were staggering. I discovered by accident how much more employees engage with the DL process when combined with the first aid for mental health training, compared to the time-consuming and admin-heavy process of staff surveys, team meetings, appraisals, and one on ones. Not that these should be ruled out, as they all still play a key role after the initial DL process.

This increased engagement with DL on courses was due to the fact that first aid for mental health courses is centred around self-care, empowering a person to look after their own mental health correctly. The training educates a person on why looking after their mental health is important and the risk factors to look out for. This is something many people who aren't mental health first aid trained struggle to grasp. The course thus creates an environment of understanding and puts everyone on the same page at a vital moment of awareness. It drives home the importance of getting mental health right, both on a personal and professional level, and that both are interconnected. This is something that can't be replicated via staff surveys, team meetings, appraisals, and one-on-ones. Therefore, the initial stage of DL is always better connected to first aid for mental health training.

With an instructor like myself as an external person creating a safe space for employees to speak their minds without the threat of retribution by a manager, employees open up much more. It's best practice not only for line managers to be present on the training courses or at the time of the DL discussion, but also for the managers above them that may never hear the everyday issues employees deal with.

Here is the full process to deliver the DL strategy.

1. Train employees in MHFA. If an entire department cannot attend together, stagger the training with no more than a few days between all staff receiving training.

2. Initiate the DL Process with these questions:

    Write three things your employer can do to help you with your wellbeing at work (keep it personal to you, your job role, and your day-to-day).

    Write three things you can do at work that can improve the wellbeing of others around you. (This can be as personal as speaking with a person who hasn't been themselves lately, all the way to changes in company policy regarding mental health and wellbeing)

3. Gather data and action quick fixes immediately, start work on other fixes and communicate with staff.

4. Use staff surveys, team meetings, appraisals and one on ones, combined with online tools and frameworks, to gather data on the following for employees:

- **Age.** Establish the age range for the department to establish possible age-specific needs and wants.
- **Financial Situation.** Establish personalised financial planning.
- **Family and Domestic Situation.** Establish any areas of support as an employer.
- **Housing Situation.** Establish living conditions and any plans that can be supported as an employer.
- **Gender Identity.** Identify and support as an employer.
- **Mental Health.** Identify any issues and support as an employer.
- **Physical Health.** Identify any issues and support as an employer.
- **Religious/Spiritual Identity.** Identify and support as an employer.
- **Disabilities.** Identify and support as an employer.
- **Resilience and Adaptability.** Establish the capacity of individuals to avoid absenteeism, presenteeism, stress, and burnout. Identify training/support needs on an individual basis.
- **Personality Type.** Establish an understanding of an employee's personality type for better personal management.
- **Experience.** Establish the capacity of individuals to set manageable targets for productivity and avoid burnout/identify training needs.

5. Use staff surveys, team meetings, appraisals, and one on ones to establish and identify suitable EAPs and management practices to meet the unique and specific requirements of each department.

The five steps of the DL process may take up to twelve months, best practice is not to let it get past eighteen months. Every three years, retrain in MHFA and repeat the DL process. Once the data is gathered, analysed and changes implemented, it will result in a much happier and more connected workforce, naturally creating people-focused management practices uniquely relevant to employees of each department.

Now, as we come to the end of this chapter and book, as a reader you would have noticed that this book is quite different from your usual people management book. I have written about the personal and the professional, connecting them to business and politics, as they are all interconnected. One thing we can be sure of is that we require a huge shift in how organisations behave, and how they manage people. The new normal has left many managers and organisations disoriented as they find their feet. The problem is that while they find their feet, humans suffer. The intention of this book is to create a new way of thinking in the workplace and to benefit from the most underrated yet most powerful facet of the working world. The human element.

This book represents new thinking for the new normal and provides a platform for a new generation of business leaders and thinkers, to benefit from the most historically undervalued, overlooked and underestimated segment in business. Human wellbeing. The value of wellbeing for organisations and economies has long been overlooked. We have come to a time in history where we need leaders who realise, a flourishing organisation can only be had via flourishing people. This book outlines an ideology that can be manufactured to help humans flourish. Flourishing and healthy humans and the benefits that manifest, both in society and in the workplace, are the true goal and essence of managing people in the new normal. It is the future of work!

Printed in Great Britain
by Amazon

39341095R00138